Land of White Gloves?

Land of White Gloves? is an important academic investigation into the history of crime and punishment in Wales. Beginning in the medieval period when the limitations of state authority fostered a law centred on kinship and compensation, the study explores the effects of the introduction of English legal models, culminating in the Acts of Union under Henry VIII. It reveals enduring traditions of extra-legal dispute settlement rooted in the conditions of Welsh Society. The study examines the impact of a growing bureaucratic state uniformity in the nineteenth century and concludes by examining the question of whether distinctive features are to be found in patterns of crime and the responses to it into the twentieth century.

Dealing with matters as diverse as drunkenness and prostitution, industrial unrest and linguistic protests, and with punishments ranging from social ostracism to execution, the book draws on a wide range of sources, primary and secondary, and insights from anthropology, social and legal history. It presents a narrative which explores the nature and development of the state, the theoretical and practical limitations of the criminal law and the relationship between law and the society in which it operates.

The book will appeal to those who wish to examine the relationships between state control and social practice and explores the material in an accessible way, which will be both useful and fascinating to those interested in the history of Wales and of the history of crime and punishment more generally.

Richard W. Ireland has been researching the history of crime and punishment for many years and has published widely in the area. Richard is a founding committee member of the Welsh Legal History Society and a member of the Board of the Centre for Welsh Legal Affairs. He has also contributed to a number of radio and television broadcasts.

History of Crime in the UK and Ireland

Series editor: Professor Barry Godfrey

Rarely do we get the opportunity to study criminal history across the British Isles, or across such a long time period. History of Crime in the UK and Ireland is a series which provides an opportunity to contrast experiences in various geographical regions and determine how these situations changed – with slow evolution or dramatic speed – and with what results. It brings together data, thought, opinion, and new theories from an established group of scholars that draw upon a wide range of existing and new research. Using case studies, examples from contemporary media, biographical life studies, thoughts and ideas on new historical methods, the authors construct lively debates on crime and the law, policing, prosecution, and punishment. Together, this series of books builds up a rich but accessible history of crime and its control in the British Isles.

Land of White Gloves?

A history of crime and punishment
in Wales

Richard W. Ireland

Routledge
Taylor & Francis Group

LONDON AND NEW YORK

First published 2015
by Routledge
2 Park Square, Milton Park, Abingdon, Oxon OX14 4RN

and by Routledge
711 Third Avenue, New York, NY 10017

Routledge is an imprint of the Taylor & Francis Group, an informa business

© 2015 Richard W. Ireland

The right of Richard W. Ireland to be identified as author of this work has been asserted by him in accordance with sections 77 and 78 of the Copyright, Designs and Patents Act 1988.

British Library Cataloguing in Publication Data
A catalogue record for this book is available from the British Library

Library of Congress Cataloging in Publication Data
Ireland, Richard W., 1955-
  Land of white gloves? : a history of crime and punishment in Wales / by Richard W. Ireland.
    pages cm. – (History of crime in the UK and Ireland ; 4)
  Includes bibliographical references.
  1. Crime–Wales–History. 2. Punishment–Wales–History. I. Title.
  HV6949.W3I74 2015
  364.9429–dc23
              2014034417

ISBN: 978-0-415-50199-6 (hbk)
ISBN: 978-0-203-06998-1 (ebk)

Typeset in Times New Roman
by Taylor & Francis Books

MIX
Paper from
responsible sources
FSC
www.fsc.org FSC® C013604

Printed and bound by CPI Group (UK) Ltd, Croydon, CR0 4YY

For my mother

Contents

Illustrations

Figures

Table

Preface

Let me start with a confession. I find it hard to finish pieces of work, to admit to myself that the time for making changes, checking facts and polishing arguments has run out. The book then goes out into the world to make its own way and to be judged for what it is, not what it might have been. Until this particular book I thought that I'd been getting a bit better at this "letting go" part of writing, but this time it hasn't been easy at all. Because it covers such a vast subject area, the book has taken me to some places and periods with which I was much less familiar than others. Academic research tends towards knowing more and more about less and less, so to find myself covering a period of over a thousand years was rather daunting. And, because it seeks to cover that ground concisely, the book also runs the risk of distortion or superficiality in its discussion, as well as simple omission. There were times when I thought that I was in danger of making a list of events ("There was another violent clash in …") rather than giving them any meaningful context. There was the occasion when I woke up from a bad night's sleep suddenly aware of the fact that I had entirely forgotten to mention the Tonypandy riots!

But this work was never for a moment intended to be a definitive history of crime and punishment in Wales, which is why I have been at such pains to press the reader to look at the footnotes and the bibliography for more specific references. I don't want to sound too apologetic here, though. The aim of the book is to fill a hole in the academic literature of crime and punishment which is as generally unnoticed as it is scandalous. The Welsh experience is interesting and important, and important no less to those outside Wales than to those within it. If it errs in the odd detail (and I sincerely hope that it doesn't) but ensures that no-one in future finds it so easy to assume that the experience of Wales was just the same as that in England, but expressed in a different accent, then it will have done its job.

I live and work in a small country, and that means that many of those who have given me assistance in researching and writing this book are personal friends as well as professional colleagues. I don't want to name them all because I'm bound to forget someone (if I can forget Tonypandy…). Many appear in footnotes, others will know who they are. So let me just say that colleagues and students, particularly my postgraduates, within my Department and more widely in the University, those in the various county archives and museums visited and contacted in the course of this research, those at the National Library of Wales, including The People's Collection, and the National Screen and Sound Archive, have been enormously generous in their willingness to help. I owe a particular debt to those individuals, organizations and institutions who allowed me to reproduce the illustrations within the text. They are credited at the appropriate place in the book, but it is important to stress that my acknowledgments are not merely formal but represent genuine gratitude. Antony Smith of Aberystwyth University's Department of Geography and Earth Sciences very kindly provided the map. My editors, initially at Willan and then, with their merger, at Routledge were splendid: Julia Willan indulged my jokes, Heidi Lee encouraged me over the line when I was getting tired and grumpy. I have personal and profound thanks to Helen and to Tammas.

Finally I want to thank the series editor, Barry Godfrey, for asking me to contribute this book to the *History of Crime in the UK and Ireland* series and thereby showing that not all who work in this area are as dismissive of the Welsh dimension as I may have suggested above. To my intense embarrassment I have not felt brave enough to discuss the project, or indeed anything else, with him since that first discussion. This is not, I should stress, due to any fierceness on his part but to exaggerated diffidence on my own. I hope that he will be pleased with this book, and that I might now finally get round to buying him a drink.

Aberystwyth
August, 2014

Map of Wales

Introduction

Why a volume on Wales? Such a defensive opening is scarcely to be expected from the authors of the other books in the series of histories of criminal justice to which this text is intended to be a contribution. Yet the jurisdictional linkage of "England and Wales" seems so well-entrenched, so natural, that a disaggregation seems gratuitous. Why not, on this basis, a volume on, say, Yorkshire? Or perhaps the separation is merely opportunistic, an example of (in that phrase which is so often used to mock an underlying desire to show respect) "political correctness" bolstered by the recognition of difference in the recent devolution settlement. This latter is, of course, very significant, and the granting of full legislative competence on particular subjects to the Government of Wales following the referendum in 2011 certainly means that it will be impossible in the future (even though I suspect that this is still but little appreciated in England) to assume that the law of the two countries will be the same. But crime and criminal justice are not areas of devolved authority, so a book intended to act as a kind of celebration of earlier difference, a kind of Whiggish "souvenir programme" for the contemporary constitutional order, would be wholly misguided. In any event there is now a gap approaching 500 years since all "sinister usages and customs" of the Welsh were abolished by a statute of Henry VIII.[1] If we seek a justification for a volume devoted to crime and reaction to it in Wales we must consider some much deeper arguments.

It is no longer academically justifiable to write a history of crime and punishment which contents itself simply with surveying the statutory or common law rules proscribing conduct, the procedures laid down for their enforcement and the practices or institutions available to address deviation from them without asking how and why those rules came about and were or were not enforced. Legal rules do not simply spontaneously generate, they come from somewhere and they go (or fail to go) somewhere. Criminal law has a particular feature which makes it demand our attention for reasons beyond the intrinsic "interest" (too seldom analysed, too seldom distinguished from prurience) which its subject material holds. It is the point at which the power of the state and the freedom of its citizen most obviously come into dramatic conflict. Crime in its essence involves the recognition that an action – an act of violence or appropriation for example – is a matter for concern for other parties than those immediately involved with that act as perpetrator and victim (let us use again the term "the state" to represent that other interest, as if the term were a simple one, although we will be obliged to consider its problematic and changing nature in a while). Indeed the interest of the state may differ from and demand different treatment from those of the more immediately involved protagonists: a victim may want the return of his property or compensation for her injury rather than the afflictive punishment deemed appropriate by the state. Nor, a point to which we will return, must it be accepted that a victim's views are necessarily those of a socially detached organism expressing purely and simply an individual rational choice, for cultural and subcultural factors may influence a response considered to be appropriate. That is not to suggest that such views will necessarily diverge, only that they may do so. This volume will have much to say about such tensions in the pages that follow.

   Let us return, however, to the question of "the state". It is impossible to enter into an exhaustive discussion of such a complex concept; neither the limited scope of this book nor the limited competence of its author will permit that. But a consideration of a number of points relating to the administration of criminal law is of particular importance in understanding why a history of that subject in Wales is both so complex and so necessary. The first question to be explored is the *capacity* of the state (by which term I seek to include both the physical capacity for intervention and the political will to accomplish it) at any particular time. A comparison may help understanding here. In England by the end of the twelfth century, following a process of development from the later Anglo-Saxon times, all serious crime (that is felony: crime punishable by death or mutilation) had become not only unamendable, that is not legally capable of being remedied by compensation, but also subject to the exclusive jurisdiction of royal courts, though lesser wrongs could still be entertained in shrieval, manorial or ecclesiastical fora. It is true that this clear conceptual position might be less rigorously maintained in practice, rape for example being a notional felony but being routinely settled by private composition either by money or marriage,[2] but there nonetheless existed a body of law enforceable in royal courts, with a machinery for prosecution theoretically independent of the victim's will and a tariff of avowedly punitive consequences for offenders. This was not the case in Wales at the same time, where, as we will see, the notion of compensation to the victim and/or the victim's kin remains uppermost. It might be thought then that the present volume should begin after the middle ages, when the dominant paradigm has become one of public rather than private wrong, or, more accurately (for a wrong may be conceived of as being one against a wider constituency than those who may enforce it), when the mechanisms of state intervention are regarded as superior to those of the individual. In fact I have eagerly pressed to be allowed to take the coverage of this book back to an earlier period than those covered in its companion volumes. This strategy, I concede, is to risk confusion or even incoherence. A book about the history of crime and punishment might be expected to base itself squarely on the notion of crime, of the sort described above in relation to English felony. The content of the criminal code may change over time, for crime is not a monolithic nor unmediated body of self-evident wrongs, but the unifying thread of public offence against state authority marks it out, as we have indicated earlier, as different from, say, the private disputes against persons. In Wales, on the other hand such clarity may not be forthcoming. "One and the same act", observes Dafydd Jenkins, "may be a sin, a crime and a personal wrong, and the law-books suggest that a court in Wales could treat the one act in the three ways at the same time".[3] Such flexibility in conceptual ordering, as will be seen below, is not to be thought of as relevant only to the earliest days of pre-conquest Wales, for we will see the persistence of communal norms of compensation even when the official paradigm of state criminality is supposedly firmly established, and see too the invocation of the rules of tenth-century kings even at a time when Wales's industry powered the industrial revolution. Accordingly it is necessary, I believe, to discuss the earlier culture in respect of the response to wrongs, and the deviation from an orthodox conception of crime in that context seems not only possible but essential. Similarly our understanding of punishment will extend at certain points in the discussion beyond the realm of state action to involve communal, individual and (perceived) eschatological punishment of social norms, which may or may not be coincident with legal ones.[4] The reader, fearing a descent into a borderless chaos, should not be alarmed. The discussion which follows should make clear when the text deviates from the comforting paradigm of state crime and punishment and, more importantly, why it has done so.

Connected with the idea of *capacity* of state is its *geographical extent*. The history of Wales, even if conceived of as the history of a geographical area rather than as the history of peoples, is not simple to trace in jurisdictional terms. A complex of different kingships and lordships was given a legal jolt in 1284 when Edward I, fresh from his defeat of Llewelyn ap Gruffudd, produced a statute which enforced (a portion) of (amended) English law to (a part of) Wales. Thereafter this system co-existed with the laws of a number of semi-autonomous Marcher lordships, whose courts applied various admixtures of traditional Welsh and borrowed English law. Not only does such a patchwork of jurisdictions make it difficult to speak unqualifiedly of a medieval law of Wales but it also raises questions as to how to characterize certain acts of violence, such as the campaign of Owain Glyn Dŵr in the fifteenth century. Is this a "treasonable revolt", a "liberation struggle" or a competition between perceived state and other legal orders? After the Union legislation of Henry VIII it might be thought that at last the problem of jurisdictional complexity had been solved, but the assimilation with the English legal system was not thereby rendered instantly complete. Separate courts continued to operate, one of which, The Council of the Principality and Marches of Wales, exercised jurisdiction also over English border counties until 1604, whilst the important superior tribunal of the Court of Great Sessions, active until abolition in 1830, excluded the Welsh county of Monmouthshire. Both institutions were of importance in relation to the administration of criminal law.

The remaining complex dynamic of state intervention is *social penetration*. Even when we are able to speak of a state able and willing to construct a criminal justice system applicable to a defined geographical ambit, we still cannot assume that its norms will automatically be the ones embraced by the people, or all of the people, within the jurisdiction. English social historians have explored those areas of "social crime", poaching, smuggling, etc., in which the ethical compasses of those enforcing the criminal law and those subjected to it might be seriously misaligned in relation to the rules enforced by the state. Social norms might be at odds with legal ones as regards the moral content of the law. Consideration of the Welsh evidence involves a further examination as to the issue of the socially perceived wisdom, propriety and utility of the invocation of legal procedures, even in cases of actions which were generally morally unambiguous, as for example, homicide. Whilst it is no part of my argument that such attitudes are restricted to Wales, I am nonetheless persuaded that they are an important facet of Welsh experience and involve elements specifically related to Welsh experience. We have seen earlier that laws have objects as well as authors, and it has been suggested that cultural factors may inform the responses of the "audience", indeed a denial of this seems impossible. Yet even in the nineteenth century, after the abolition of separate courts had made an unequivocally uniform official legal system, the Welsh (I speak in generalities, which will be refined later) neither saw themselves as the same as the English, nor were seen to be so by the English. Language, religion and long-standing customs of dispute resolution and social sanctions were all different from those of the English, and different from those characteristics as they were enshrined within the official legal system of England "and Wales". This is not to assert that such social and cultural factors inform all events of crime and the responses to them which are to be found in Wales, nor inform them to the same effect and in the same way across individuals, across geographical and other communities and across time in the same way and to the same extent. There is no simple element within the water of Wales (and if there were we would presumably have to follow it through the pipes into Birmingham and Liverpool!) which "explains" and differentiates the motivation, morphology and reaction to all aspects of offending in Wales, although we will come across writers in the nineteenth century who come close to such a proposition. But anyone who believes that there is a social dimension to the history of crime and punishment must surely acknowledge the importance of such profoundly important social markers as, *inter alia*, language, religion and custom in formulating and expressing cultural norms and touching individual actions. Anyone who does not believe in such a dimension is urged to stop reading this work at this point and attempt to get a refund from their bookshop before they risk despoiling any further pages.

If the starting point of this survey presents some problems, then so too does its finishing point. For the variables of state capacity, geographical reach (subject to the recent complication of devolution) and social penetration seem, frankly, applicable in no markedly different a manner today than they are in England. The pioneering historian of Welsh crime, D.J.V. Jones, wrote in his sadly unfinished review of policing in South Wales in the twentieth century that, with some specific exceptions, "there was not a permanently and distinctly Welsh character to the delinquency described in this book".[5] The same could be said, I think, of the institutional response. This assimilation in itself is interesting for it raises the question as to whether it is a more efficient penetration of a more uniform nation state (as for example evidenced by the greater collaboration between police forces or the nationalization of the prison system), a loosening of geographical specificity of criminality (as the car and the computer dissolve the physical nexus between offence and offender) or a greater cultural homogeneity (where "national" characteristics are more formally ascribed to legislatures or sporting teams than inductively derived from normative practice[6]) or any combination of these which underlies it. To such matters we will return in due course, but there is a specific reason for mentioning them here. For there is a danger in straining to find difference in more recent experience which may distort a wider picture of criminality. It would be entirely wrong to ignore the issues of disorder associated with industrial unrest in twentieth-century Wales or the holiday-home arson campaign, but wrong too to write of these as simply representative of Welsh criminality in that period. It would be wrong for another reason too, for I have argued elsewhere, and not in relation to Welsh material alone, that the concentration on serious offences and condign punishment in a large proportion of even scholarly criminal historiography is responsible for misrepresentation of the lived experience of the past.[7] Drunkenness, petty theft and driving offences must be studied as well as riot and murder, and the recognizance and the fine as much as hanging and transportation. There are certain practical difficulties, some evidential (an absence of easily available records) some self-proliferating (the hidden agenda of the dramatic which may help explain why such records as do exist are not more easily available). Nonetheless it is important to state at the outset that this study will seek to encompass the trivial and mundane aspects of criminality and the response to it as well as the terrible.

Even if we consider earlier periods, it is not necessary to maintain the absolute uniqueness of Welsh experience in order to justify the present volume. When the specific native laws of the medieval period alone are looked at, undoubtedly geographically rooted as they are, there may exist at times intriguing parallels in Irish or in Anglo-Saxon texts. As to the later period it is not my contention that local customs of, say, dispute settlement could be at odds with law only in Wales, for the literature makes plain, and I have already conceded, that such normative collisions are also to be found in England, particularly perhaps in rural England.[8] Yet the case for a criminal history which deals specifically with Wales, as indeed with other aspects of "social history", remains compelling. As the specific variables of state involvement identified above and to be further considered in the following discussion make plain, the variance from practice elsewhere will be seen at some times to be clearly marked and at others to be differently mediated and differently nuanced. And by "elsewhere" I mean principally, of course, England. Welsh crime and criminality (and the historical antecedents to such categories), though as far as I know they have never before supported a monograph of the kind offered here, have certainly had their investigators and commentators, notably Dafydd Jenkins, Morfydd Owen, Beverly and Llinos Beverly Smith, Thomas Charles-Edwards and others on the medieval material, and J. Gwynfor Jones, Murray Chapman, Sharon Howard, David Howell and D.J.V. Jones and others on more recent material. I have myself written on both early and nineteenth-century matters. Yet the work, I suspect, has never fully penetrated the mainstream of criminal historiography. The experience of Wales seems to be regarded as either inexplicably different to the position in England or as unproblematically the same, or (and I suspect that this is the most common position) it is simply not considered at all. This seems to me indefensible. The understanding of crime has long since extended beyond a simple doctrinal analysis of offences to incorporate an analysis of its position in social structures and mentalities. To fail to explore these insofar as they relate to minorities (linguistic, religious, cultural) of considerable size and constitutional significance is to conceal very important developments. It must be stressed that these developments are not those which relate to the minority culture only: they have a genuine and important role to play in explaining the more dominant one. Let us take a relatively recent example to make the point. There was a major redrafting of traditional responsibilities for and responses to crime and punishment in the nineteenth century. Public order is (I'm not going to go into the details here: the essence of the argument seems to me incontrovertible in outline) being transformed from a local to a national concern, prosecution from an individual to an organized phenomenon, trial from an unstructured to a rule-dominated process, punishment from a physical to a carceral experience. Underneath all lay (in the Webbs' still-important phrase) the "fetish of uniformity". To regard these transitions from the point of view of those who were their (reluctant? obstructive?) local instruments is to illuminate the very processes themselves, not simply peripheral reactions to them.

There are other issues of "Welshness" to be addressed before the chapters which follow. First it must be stressed that this is a history of crime and punishment in Wales, rather than that involving Welsh actors. That decision seems reasonable, but, if we are right in urging social and cultural factors as having a bearing on these issues, is perhaps just a little less reasonable than it looks. Nonetheless, whilst some might be interested to read of the activities of Welsh criminals acting outside Wales (Renwick Williams perhaps, the celebrity sex offender who brought terror to the streets of eighteenth-century London as "The Monster", or the international exploits of notorious drug trafficker Howard Marks) or of their equivalents in law enforcement (the career of "hanging judge" George Jeffreys, or that of Nuremberg prosecutor Elwyn Jones) they will be obliged to look elsewhere.[9] In relation to language within the text, Welsh terms are retained, after explanation, when they are of a technical nature (*sarhaed* for example, for insult) and quotations from earlier sources will, of course, retain the original spellings. As for proper names of persons or towns I will employ whichever version seems more justifiable in context – Llewellyn ap Gruffudd or Caernarfon, for example, but not Caerdydd (Cardiff) or Abertawe (Swansea). Such hybridity may seem discordant (and perhaps principally reflects the discomfort of an English author who has lived most of his life in Wales), but it is, I think, justified by the desire to make the text readily accessible.

A note too is necessary on methodology. This study will, of course, involve some statistical evidence relating to the incidence of crime, but the current volume is not predominantly a statistical one. The problems of using official figures of criminality, both in contemporary and, *a fortiori*, historical analysis are now sufficiently well known; I hope that a protracted discussion of them is not necessary. In relation to medieval Welsh law it is often only the texts of the Laws themselves or those of a literary nature which inform our knowledge, rather than any records of court proceedings. Early modern proceedings are better preserved, but such procedures as counting of indictments are marked by potential difficulty.[10] The nineteenth century produced, for the first time, a modern statistical approach to measuring crime and that innovation is a most important one, as much for the conceptions which underlie the enterprise as for the figures which it produced. Jones has discussed and utilized these figures in his work and I have no wish to reproduce that process here.[11] In a study which will return at a number of points to the practice of extracurial settlements of wrong and which provides a narrative which for the most part precedes the institution of the police (as both "disinterested" prosecutors of crime and the recorders of it) and the type of information provided in recent years by the British Crime Survey, a qualitative approach to evidence will dominate. This of course is, in itself, not without difficulty, for the reader may fall victim to an unarticulated bias or distortion introduced by the author which is the more pernicious, because less explored, than the well-rehearsed arguments concerning the deficiencies of statistics. Such distortion might lie, as I have hinted at above, in the temptation to select the atypical information (because eye-catchingly serious, distinctively Welsh or entertainingly strange) and to present it as representing the norm. I will try to avoid such a temptation, although I cannot promise, particularly in relation to the last category, always to do so. It would take a harder heart than I have, or perhaps simply a more disciplined scholar, to avoid mentioning, for example, the uproar caused in Carmarthen by the mesmerized band controlled by Mrs Poole in 1868, although it has, in truth, little to tell us of quotidian criminality.[12] On a more serious note though it must be accepted that there is no way that a criminal history, any criminal history, can be reduced to a recital of "mere facts" unmediated by authorial influence. The assembly of narrative connections, the interpretation of events and their significance, are matters of judgement. To take a well-known example, the replacement of the "Bloody Code" of capital offences by a justice system largely dependent on the use of imprisonment may be, has been, variously presented as a triumph of humanitarianism, an outgrowth of industrial capitalism, a key instance of a new, pervasive concept of governance or a response to population growth and demographic change.[13] I will try to indicate (and the use of the first person should remind the reader of the possibility throughout) where my interpretations might be seen as out of line with more orthodox opinion or where alternative explanations have significant support. In the end, however, this remains *a* history of crime and punishment in Wales. It cannot claim to be *the* history.

I have, however, been entirely orthodox in adopting a largely chronological approach to the subject. This would seem to be in line with both settled expectations and the way that readers might expect to use this book, for some will no doubt be particularly interested in "their" period and will therefore expect to find it. Yet it is banal to observe that, although major events may have profound consequences (in our context, for example, the Edwardian or Henrician legislation), history seldom arranges itself around clean breaks. In a work of this kind, which will have cause to remark on certain continuities, such as extra-curial compensation or robust jury independence, to use the chronological method is to run the risk of missing this focus. Accordingly I will return to these themes as the work unfolds and hope that the reader will forgive the clunky "as we have seen also in the seventeenth century" which such an exercise entails. One further note on style is needed. The publishers require that endnotes rather than footnotes should accompany the texts. The notes to this volume contain not simply references but also, at times, illustrations which accompany the argument but which might (and in particular perhaps in those instances where their inclusion is unashamedly to give life or colour) detract from the clarity of argument. They are easy to ignore where they are, but the reader may enjoy some of them. I hope also that they, together with the bibliography, will give an indication of the richness of material, published and archival, relating to Wales which is still too often ignored by historians of crime and punishment outside its boundaries.

Finally I must explain the title of this book. It was the custom to hand to the judge on Assize a pair of white gloves if that sitting was a "maiden" one, that is, which presented no serious crime to be tried. This, as we shall see, was not as rare in Wales as might be imagined, and the self-identification of "*gwlad y menig gwynion*" ("the land of white gloves") became a potent symbol of Welsh probity.[14] Similarly in 1873 *The Graphic* reproduced a picture of the county gaol at Beaumaris on Anglesey, flying a white flag and with its doors standing open, there being no prisoners confined within.[15] If the message of gloves and flag is to be believed, it may be difficult to find enough material to fill a book on crime and punishment in Wales. I have not, however, found it difficult. The image of Wales as crime-free becomes then a matter for a more nuanced analysis within the narrative, rather than a reason to abandon the project at the outset!

Notes

1 27 Hen.VIII c.26, s.1.
2 See on this R.W. Ireland, "Lucrece, Philomela (and Cecily): Chaucer and the law of rape" in T. Haskett (ed.) *Crime and Punishment in the Middle Ages* (Victoria: University of Victoria, 1998) pp. 37–61. This volume contains a number of essays on the English medieval system, but for an overview see, e.g., J.H. Baker, *An Introduction to English Legal History* (4th edn, London: Butterworths, 2002) Ch. 29.
3 D. Jenkins, "Crime and tort and the three columns of law" in T. Charles-Edwards and P. Russell (eds) *Tair Colofn Cyfraith: The Three Columns of Law in Medieval Wales* (Bangor: The Welsh Legal History Society, 2005) p. 1.
4 The approach to punishment in this work is informed by the reconceptualization of the idea to be found in C. Harding and R.W. Ireland, *Punishment: Rhetoric, Rule and Practice* (London: Routledge, 1989).
5 D.J.V. Jones, *Crime and Policing in the Twentieth Century: The South Wales Experience* (Cardiff: University of Wales Press, 1996) p. 287.
6 This in itself may be part of a wider process of "disembeddedness" which the criminologist Jock Young regards as one of the key changes of late modernity. See his *The Criminological Imagination* (Malden, MA: Polity, 2011) Ch. 5.
7 See, e.g., R.W. Ireland, "'A second Ireland'? Crime and popular culture in nineteenth-century Wales" in R. McMahon (ed.) *Crime, Law and Popular Culture in Europe since 1500* (Cullompton: Willan, 2008) p. 239.
8 The point is one to which we will return; for now it will be sufficient to cite by way of example E.P. Thompson's well-known collection *Customs in Common* (London: Merlin, 1991).
9 For Williams, see J. Bonderson (2001) *History Today*, May, p. 30; for Marks, see his own *Mr Nice* (London: Vintage, 1996); for Jeffreys, see http://yba.llgc.org.uk/en/s-JEFF-GEO-1645.html; for Elwyn Jones, see www.archiveswales.org.uk/anw/get_collection.php?inst_id=1&coll_id=264&expand=.
10 For a discussion, see P. Rawlings in W.D. Hines (ed.) *English Legal History: A Bibliography and Guide to the Literature* (New York: Garland, 1990) pp. 88–91.
11 D.J.V. Jones, *Crime in Nineteenth-Century Wales* (Cardiff: University of Wales Press, 1992). This admirable volume warns of the dangers of the statistical method, yet uses the technique with rather more boldness than I would myself employ.
12 Infra, p. 69.
13 See R.W. Ireland, *"A Want of Order and Good Discipline": Rules, Discretion and the Victorian Prison* (Cardiff: University of Wales Press, 2007) pp. 7–32.
14 Infra, p. 60.
15 *The Graphic*, 15 November 1873.

1 The middle ages

Victims, lords and kings

Few subjects can seem more resistant to accurate synopsis than the history of medieval Wales with all the complexities of its geographical and temporal variety, few subjects within that history more resistant to understanding than the mutable and sometimes opaque provisions of its law texts, few legal worlds more in need of practical rather than normative evidence to explain the relationship between what the law said and what it did. No attempt will be made within this chapter to resolve those difficulties in a way that would satisfy the serious scholar of medieval Welsh History. Yet, as suggested in the introduction, the decision to go back to the middle ages within this book is one that has been made quite deliberately, regardless of the dangers inherent in that enterprise. The reasons need to be stated at the outset, for they must be borne in mind throughout this text and not merely in this chapter. Simply put, then, we start with some historical evidence which will underline the basic proposition that Welsh experience is not simply English experience with a rather different accent. Second we will learn that the provisions of "the criminal law" are both plastic and pragmatic, varying over time and place, drawing from both native custom and neighbouring practice, generally for reasons relating to what is possible and or desirable (for disputants, "the authorities" or both) rather than those of intellectual coherence. This will remind us too that in later chapters, even where the ambit of the criminal law is apparently geographically and temporally certain, it will not always prevail in the face of other arguments. Finally, and related to this last point, the argument briefly made in the introduction, that the nexus of wrongdoing involves three parties, the wrongdoer, the victim and the public authority (and the use of three singular nouns here in itself may be an oversimplification of the position in reality), displays a powerful interconnection of interests which is subject to dispute and renegotiation: a factor as important to recognize in the twenty-first century as much as in the twelfth.

Medieval native Welsh law was, unlike its English counterpart, the law of the book, customary rules being reduced to writing by and for a juristic class, its origins and nature elegantly described as lying in "truth, conscience and learning".[1] The law as a whole takes its generic name, *Cyfraith Hywel* (the Laws of Hywel), from the king with whom this process of compilation was associated, who traditionally bears the appellation Hywel Dda ("Hywel the Good"), who died in 949 or 950. Hywel had, unusually and briefly, gained Kingship over a number of traditionally independent areas of Wales, and the law, despite the fact that it is known to us only through later manuscripts belonging to no fewer than three distinct textual traditions, contains some essential features which are of interest to us. These manuscripts come from the late twelfth and thirteenth centuries, and versions exist both in native Welsh and in the international language of the middle ages, Latin. Before the advent of printing, the production of a text was not an event but a process, during the course of which later additions and deletions were introduced into existing traditions, depending on temporal changes, the geographical provenance or applicability of the text and, we must assume, other more disparate reasons. It is only in the relatively recent past that the texts of native Welsh law have received the detailed analysis and academic commentary they so richly deserve, but my task here is not to add depth to that analysis and commentary (even if I were capable of it: I am not), but to examine the overall picture of the legal response to wrongdoing which the laws prescribe and to try and establish a context for their operation.[2]

As in many societies to be found both historically and in contemporary anthropological literature the importance of the kindred group to early Welsh social organization was notable, as an obvious, "natural" and to an extent determinable nucleus of support and defence for an individual. A wrong to that individual was, typically, construed as a wrong to the kindred as well, just as a liability might also be seen as a communal, not simply an individual, burden. This long survives as a characteristic feature of Welsh medieval law, as we shall see, but it is perhaps worth noting that such a wrong need not be seen as *exclusively* a wrong to the individual and his or her kin. The temptation to confuse the limitations of the enforcement mechanism of *redress* for wrong with the absence of a wider social dimension to the *concept* of that wrong, even before lords or kings take a role in intervention, is not always one which is resisted, though it is not a necessary elision. If someone murders your brother in defiance of hospitality, or steals your sheep, that does not mean, simply because the reaction to that wrong is believed to be a matter for you and your kin, that I too will not think it is wrong, a breach of communal standards, rather than some kind of breach of a personal contract between family groups: *ex hypothesi* it cannot be, or the general norms underlying the specific rules could not exist. But there are good reasons for the kindred group to have such enforcement rights and obligations ascribed to them in societies in which a specialist function of rule-enforcement, with the necessity of division of labour and a system of rewards and of status sufficient to underpin that function, is lacking or undeveloped. As to the morphology of response to wrongdoing, then simple equivalence is as intelligible as it is economical: the retaliation with violence on the violent, the removal of the protection of societal norms from those who have broken those norms, needs little in the way of sophisticated apparatus. But a moment's thought reveals that such "talionic" penalties are not precise but only approximate in their equivalence. So, for example, the individual that I kill may be your brother, but he may be a worse warrior, or farmer, or a bigger drunk than I am, and when you come looking for me, the talented only-child who is his family's support and hope, that approximate equivalence of one life for another may not entirely satisfy the balance, leaving a sense of outrage or injustice. The problem which inheres in any system of reciprocated violence, then, is that it may not heal social discord but may actually increase it, dragging in other actors and sometimes extending for generations. Functionally it is wise to have an alternative to physical retaliation to restore relations to the satisfaction of all concerned, and again the enforcement rights and obligations of the kindred group limit in practical terms what that alternative might be.[3] Traditionally the alternative to, and termination of, violence is to be found in compensation, where not only is the dispute ended, but it is ended (for it operates on a different plane to that which appeals simply to warrior virtue) without compromise to honour. So it is in medieval Wales. The essentially structural understanding of the nature of these dispute settlement techniques should put us on guard against any anachronistic reading of medieval Welsh law as representing a more enlightened and humane code than that of others. It may be considered by later commentators to have been so, but such conceptions were not its formative roots.

Let us consider the law of homicide as an example of the process. The Welsh word "*galanas*", used *inter alia* to describe the compensation for this offence is etymologically derived from the concept of "enmity" to which, as we have seen, the idea of compensation is an alternative.[4] Another word for "enmity" often used in this precise context is "feud" and such a usage is so familiar that it may be properly used, as long as it is remembered that the resort to inter-kindred retaliation so termed is not necessarily open-ended or inevitable, nor yet is it wholly unstructured insofar as it operates in a context of social and legal norms, unlike a looser, less technical notion of enduring violence which the term might connote. It is in order to keep this context in mind that the formulation "customary vengeance" might be preferable.[5] Of course the laws themselves say little about the actual conduct of the violence beyond the analysis of relevant kindred structure, for the former is, of necessity, a practical matter: the law's role is to regulate the alternative, the compensation payment. In this respect the nature of Welsh law is similar to, amongst others, early Irish, Anglo-Saxon and Icelandic codes.

In (overtly, though not only in those!) status-based societies, of course, not all individuals are considered to be equal in value. To kill a king or a nobleman is to incur a liability to pay more than to kill a woman or a slave. It is the task of the law to assign an appropriate payment for such loss of life, *galanas*, in this specific sense, and also the range of persons who were liable to pay, and their respective liabilities, based on their kin relationship to the wrongdoer. Normally, as might be expected in such societies, the original measure of value was to be found not in money but in livestock.

As with so many aspects of medieval Welsh law the operation of the system of compensation in practice is not easy to discover. There are certainly instances where we see a payment being made closely adhering to that formally laid down in the legal texts, but anthropological evidence, and that of other historical societies, suggests that it is not improbable that the sums laid down in the books may have been used in other cases as "default" positions: sums that could be insisted upon if the parties have failed to negotiate their own settlements.[6] The laws prescribe sums which differ not only with the status of the victim but also with the degree of culpability of the offender. Thomas Charles-Edwards, in an acute analysis of a dispute considered in the collection of tales we know as the *Mabinogion*, points out that settlement of disputes, restoration of harmony, is the important end to be achieved, the law playing an important role in this process, but not the only or necessarily decisive one.[7] The same communal element of life which involved wider parties in the collection and receipt of compensation might also see an offence as involving the actions of a number of different wrongdoers, the responsibility being that of an *affaeth* in the texts, an accessory in modern legal parlance. Their culpability is marked in objective terms: one who holds the victim for the killer is more blameworthy, and will pay more, than one who accompanies the killer to the scene of the crime, and both are more heavily liable than one who merely points that victim out.[8] Interestingly, no doubt to avoid the danger of "horizontal" extension of the state of feud, these accessories are liable to the king for their wrong, but not to the kindred. Here again we see that a notion of wrong being essentially justiciable by one body does not prevent it being seen as also involving an offence to others.[9]

There is a further complication with homicide. We have seen it above used to illustrate the link between wrong, feud and compensation. *Galanas* is the term used to describe the value of the victim's death, what in Anglo-Saxon England was called "wergild", or "man-price". But it was not only life that was attacked when a man was killed, it was the attribute that was inextricably connected with that life (and indeed was instrumental in the calculation of *galanas*), his honour. Because of this, a payment, called *sarhaed* (sometimes, interestingly, *wyneberth* – "worth of face"), was payable for the affront in addition to, indeed in advance of, the *galanas* in cases of killing, and was payable outside homicide for a range of wrongs, from assault to adultery. Honour, another status attribute, varied according to rank and sex, and again the regulation of such payments was a principal task of the law. A famous example from the laws reveals that the *sarhaed* of the King of Aberffraw, if shamed "in respect of his wife", comprises:

> a gold plate for him, as broad as his face and as thick as the nail of a ploughman who has been a ploughman nine years; and a gold rod as long as himself and as thick as his little finger, and a hundred cows for every cantred [a unit of land] that he has, with a white bull with red ears for every hundred cows among them.

The *sarhaed* of a slave, more humbly but no less evocatively, is set at a pound for himself and a further twelve pence for his accoutrements, "six for a smock and three for breeches and one for a rope and one for a hedging bill and one for brogues".[10]

It will have become clear that the customary rules recorded in the law texts, or at any rate those that go furthest back into Welsh history, have little to say about the role of public authorities in the enforcement of the law. Those most acquainted with customs, which were originally oral and subsequently written, may have advised on their nature and content, or important individuals, secular or religious, may have influenced the resolution of disputes, but of "state" involvement in prosecution and punishment of crime there is little evidence in our earliest records. Insofar as early Welsh kings or other lords played any active role in killing and robbery it was as participants rather than enforcement agencies, although in the former capacity we do sometimes find them paying compensation for their own wrongs, particularly to the church, as did King Tewdwr of Brycheiniog in the early tenth century. More surprisingly perhaps, we learn of the fabulous King Arthur actually receiving compensation after a wrongful intervention by St Cadog.[11] Yet the duties of kings in respect of the protection of their peoples were primarily conceived of as addressing outside threats, not internal disorder, despite the expectation of Gildas as early as the sixth century that kings would pursue thieves and punish wrongdoers. There are signs of development, however. We find reference in some texts to an "enforcing third" of the compensation payable to the lord for his enforcement of the action, whilst, in South Wales at any rate, secret homicide, a particularly grave offence, could in some cases result in the death penalty.[12]

It should be remembered, however, that the king was not the only "public authority" in medieval society, for the church too had an obvious interest in the spiritual welfare of its members. As a result, as we shall see, it offered not only its protection to individuals but also its correction. Penance for murder could be for as long as 13 years.[13]

The power and responsibilities of medieval "states" (the word begs a lot of questions, yet the formulation "kingship" suggests a purely individual administration which might serve to ignore the wider administrative, social and legal developments which were at issue, as well as the more obvious issue in Wales of a proliferation of lordships) were not static. Nor were they isolated, and experiences in other jurisdictions could act as models for change at home. The evidence of the Welsh law books indicates an increasing intervention in dispute by authority outside the kindred group, which nevertheless left some of the essence of the old compensation system intact, although alongside that change there seems evidence too that the kindred is declining in their role of contributors to compensation payments as opposed to recipients thereof. It seems that, in compensation, as in punishment, a model of individual guilt rather than familial responsibility is gaining ground.[14]

We must be a little wary about assuming *ab initio* that the formulation of a new rule implies responsibility for its execution: to maintain that the

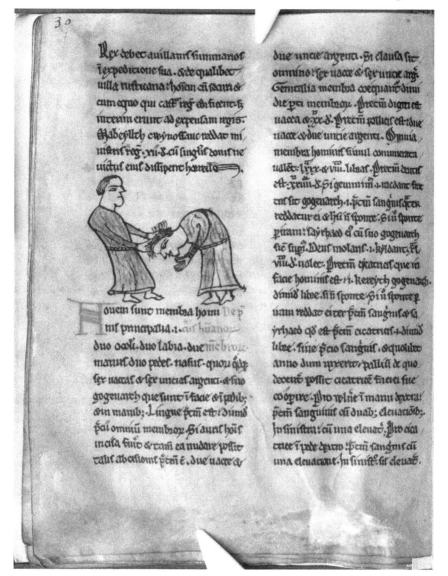

Figure 1.1 Sarhaed by hair-pulling from a thirteenth-century Latin text of Welsh
medieval law, possibly the copy owned by Archbishop Pecham (Peniarth
28, fol 15v) who was critical of content of the laws.
By permission of Llyfrgell Genedlaethol Cymru/National Library of Wales.

increasing use of afflictive punishment for wrongs (death, exile, etc.) rather than simply emendation to the kin *may* indicate a developing conception that "crime" is a matter which touches communities more than individuals, but it does not in itself imply that any defined body of state functionaries charged with executing the judgments is necessarily in existence. Nonetheless it is clear that, as the middle ages progressed, dispute settlement becomes a matter which increasingly involves authority outside the kindred. Courts play a larger role and punishment sits alongside compensation as a response to wrongdoing.

The law of theft seems to be a good example of this process. The general argument advanced above is supported by more detailed investigation of the textual sources to suggest that movement occurs in the direction which we would expect,[15] for theft, like other wrongs, bears both a public and a private face, and it is a constant and widespread danger. On the one hand it creates a personal loss in the victim, on the other its secrecy undermines social trust and presents thereby grave social danger, perhaps more urgently so than other more overt and more immediately individual wrongs.[16] It is in this way, as marking the communal danger of unattributable wrongoing, that we can understand the statement in one of the sources that theft is "everything done which is denied".[17] So we find the development of a series of afflictive sanctions, those, in other words, which dramatize the wrong of an action rather than the indebtedness which it creates as between the immediate parties. Again it is unnecessary here to go into details, but the texts make reference to a range of punishments to which theft, in different circumstances, may give rise: a fine payable to the lord (*dirwy*), enslavement, exile or death. We also hear of another sanction. A thief executed for his offence (and a refinement attributed to the eleventh century makes it clear that such a penalty is to be imposed only when the value of the stolen goods is greater than four pence) is not entitled to be buried in consecrated ground.[18] We should note, and it is a point to which we will return again, that spiritual and eschatological penalties are by no means unimportant in an age of faith.

In England the realignment of the law of wrongs away from being a matter of primary concern to the parties had come earlier and, officially at any rate, much more comprehensively than in Wales. By the time of Henry II's reign in the later twelfth century a sophisticated system of criminal courts meting out afflictive punishments was firmly established within England. The clash between Llewelyn ap Gruffudd and Edward I, which had ended in a defeat for the Welsh in 1282, brought into relief the difference between legal systems. Edward famously investigated Welsh law before imposing his settlement by statute (the Statute of Wales or Statute of Rhuddlan of 1284[19]), allowing some customary rules, abolishing some and "correcting" others. In relation to criminal law, perhaps unsurprisingly in view of the hostile animadversions of his Archbishop of Canterbury,[20] Edward adopted an essentially English pattern, establishing coroners and sheriffs with their courts (the list of matters provided for the latter to investigate is a full one, heavy with provisions in relation to agricultural crime). The statute as a whole is infused with the notion of criminal law; in its form it reads like the escheat, i.e. the forfeiture of land to the lord which in English law is a consequence of the conviction of a criminal tenant. Though it contains provisions which look, in a context of English law of the time, rather antiquated (in its measures concerning both rape and "handhaving" thieves who are taken in the act), the statute decisively turns its back, as a matter of principle, on the regime of compensation, underlining this antagonism by a specific provision against compounding actions for theft.

It must be emphasized, however, that this did not mean that all of Wales was henceforth applying English-style rules and procedures. Yet again we have to be aware of the two limitations, in terms of geographical extent and social penetration, on conjuring a simple notion of the medieval state. The Edwardian legislation applied to the lands of Llewelyn and his allies in North and West Wales, leaving a number of largely autonomous Marcher Lordships with their own courts applying their own laws. As to the latter, the perceptive Rees Davies warns us at the outset to expect difficulty if we look for geographical unity, temporal stability or homogeneity of juristic approach:

> The law of the March … was a compound of archaic practices, of feudal and local customs, of English writs and statutes and procedural methods and of a not inconsiderable body of Welsh law. It was not a uniform body of law.[21]

Even within a lordship there might be different processes for Welsh and English inhabitants, many of the latter being dominant within urban centres. As to the second limitation, that of social acceptance and employment of the English laws, we would do well to remember that, even within those territories to which they applied, custom, and particularly custom which responds well to the needs of the society in which it operates, is not necessarily expunged by the entry of some words upon the statute roll. Both of these matters require further consideration.

The borders of the March, which had been fluid and determined at any one time by the "flow of historical events"[22] rather than by more jurisprudential considerations, became more settled after 1300. Lords had the right to try and to pardon all offences short of treason.[23] But the law as enforced seems to have drawn on both native tradition and the models used in England without any overriding principle, save perhaps the increase of powers of lords which the English system with its paradigm of central authority would favour, when they felt strong enough to chance their arms. In substantive law, then, the old compensation model seems to have long survived, even where, as in the northern lordship of Dyffryn Clwyd, it seems to have existed procedurally alongside the English-based criminal prosecution procedure of the appeal of felony.[24] The same lordship, and others, seems also to have shown a willingness to maintain a degree of protection from violence for women, traditional in Welsh but regarded as less a matter for litigation in English law.[25]

Juries, no part of the native Welsh law of proof (which traditionally used the solemn oath, often sworn on relics, as its means of settling disputes instead), come to be found in the lordships. Sometimes their use was provided to a litigant as a purchasable favour, but gradually it developed as a more regular and settled procedure, even in cases of *sarhaed* and *galanas*. The process of "peine forte et dure" was also known.[26] This was the pressing of a suspect under weights to compel him to "choose" a jury when he refused to do so voluntarily, for paradoxically English law long required the defendant's consent if he was to subject himself to the trial of his peers rather than the judgment of God. Afflictive punishments, from the "cucking stool" to the pillory and the scaffold are to be found in operation in the later middle ages.[27] As to the latter, we have one of our fullest and most remarkable accounts of any medieval execution relating to the hanging of John Cragh in 1290. Cragh had apparently risen from the dead after his execution by William de Briouze, Lord of the Marcher Lordship of Gower, by a miracle attributed to Thomas Canteloupe. An investigation into this claim, as part of a papal inquiry to determine whether Canteloupe should be canonized, has left a splendid record behind. The intermingling of English and Welsh legal traditions can be detected in the evidence recorded as being presented by William de Briouze Junior who reported that "It is the custom in the land of Wales that those who are about to be hanged can escape with a payment if the temporal lords who have sentenced them to be hanged agree". In this case the lord had refused an offer from the kinsmen of Cragh and his fellow convict of 100 cows, rather more than might have been anticipated from the native law texts.[28]

Although we have been concentrating on the position of the March in the later middle ages, where lords, protective of their independence, might jealously defend their jurisdictional privileges,[29] it would be naïve to suppose that, even in those areas supposedly employing an Anglicized procedure, the old ways were forgotten. Such survivals of older process, as we will have cause to remark on many occasions within this book, are not necessarily to be understood simply as an atavistic rejection of a new legal order or an indication of an anarchic disposition. Dispute settlement techniques work for as long as they work, and in the social circumstances in which the conditions for their existence prevail. Law is an instrument which is of great importance, particularly in the modern world, but its use will require that those who are supposed to employ it both know of its existence and choose to employ it above other instruments available to them. We need not assume that these conditions will automatically apply in the Wales of the middles ages, or indeed later.

Secular law was not the only constraining factor on behaviour in medieval Wales. In a society imbued with religion, the strictures of such law might not even be the most significant means of control: as the great medievalist Marc Bloch reminds us, we must "recognize in the fear of hell one of the great social forces of the age".[30] The laws of kings, lords and the church operated together, though here again the balance of authority was stable neither temporally nor geographically. Generally as time went on the claims of lay powers, for example to take the chattels of convicted felons, encroached on those of the church, whose rights seem to have been placed under more pressure in North Wales than in the south. Procedurally, as we have noted, the oath on gospels or relics placed religion at the very heart of domestic secular law. This was so even though the testing of that oath by invocation of divine intervention in trial by ordeal was unknown to the tradition, save as an Anglo-Norman borrowing in the March or as a form of folk practice which survived even into the nineteenth century.[31] We have seen too that penance was regarded as part of the armoury of response to wrongdoing, as was excommunication, the spiritual equivalent of the temporal penalty of banishment. The church also had distinct and important privileges. Its priests claimed the right, which proved so controversial within England in the twelfth century, to be tried in ecclesiastical courts, even when that might still, apparently, result in compensation being paid. The church also provided through the doctrine of sanctuary an exemption, originally it seems as a personal grant but subsequently as attached to a territorial rea which might be of a considerable extent, from the feud or from the legal proceedings which we have seen replacing it. Lack of respect for the rights of the church could result in death, as the seventh-century burial stone of one Idnert in the church at Llanddewi Brefi makes clear.[32] The carrying of relics also seems to have been accepted as an insurance against violence, not only on a miraculous basis, but also as indicative of the jurisdictional power and protection of the church.[33] But it was not only the church which could invoke the intervention of the extra-human in disputes. We know that, in the middle ages, and later, malefactors could be cursed by individuals such as their victims.[34] It is, of course, impossible to judge the efficacy of such interventions. The long survival of such practices alongside others, notably as with those used to recover stolen goods, which rely on such direct appeals to supernatural agency argues strongly that they were taken seriously by those who employed them, and probably by those against whom they were invoked.

Other control agencies and mechanisms deserve brief mention if we are to consider the full range of responses to behaviour regarded as deviant rather than restricting ourselves to an anachronistic concentration on the criminal law in a modern sense. We know, for example, that Guilds regulated their members and could exercise disciplinary functions.[35] Lords, too, could discipline their subordinates extra-curially, sometimes using the kind of crudely symbolic shaming punishments which are often met in societies in which an individual's "character" is regarded not simply as a personal quality but as a public construction.[36] Both the use of the workplace as a means of controlling behaviour and the use of shaming as a methodology remain important, as later chapters will testify, long beyond the middle ages.

So far this discussion has concentrated upon the structure of the law and the procedures employed to deal with behaviour which, to modern readers, would fall within the ambit of the criminal law. In an age before criminal statistics or self-report studies it is obviously difficult to find any reliable evidence of the amount of violence, dishonesty and the like within medieval Welsh society or to determine how it compared to other societies at the time. The anecdotal evidence remains exactly that and is no doubt informed by the standpoint of the writer. Gerald of Wales, writing at the end of the twelfth century, had no doubt that foreign subjugation of the Welsh was a punishment for their vices, among which he enumerated "perjuries, thefts, robberies, plunderings, murders and fratricides, adulteries and incests".[37] Much later, Henry VIII's legislators, keen, as will be seen, to assimilate the diversity of Welsh legal systems into the English model, similarly provided a list of failings characterized by their breadth rather than any claim to analytical depth; the people of Wales and the Marches, we are told, "have of longe tyme contynued and persevered yn perpetracion and commysssion of dyvers and manye folde theftes, murders, rebellyons, wilfull burninge of Houses and other scelerous Dedes and abhomynable malifactes".[38]

The idea that malefactors might avoid justice by skipping over the border into a different jurisdiction (of England, the Principality, or another lord), even where it did happen, was probably viewed initially as less inherently worrying to medieval minds than it is today. For this was an age whose laws still spoke of banishment as a form of punishment and whose penalties more widely were often marked, in the compelling phrase used by Summerson to describe practice in England in this period, by principles of "publicity and exclusion". Yet, as we will see shortly, the issue became increasingly difficult to accept (or increasingly useful to project) as pressure developed towards a single nation state. We certainly know that people did flee justice; a group of apparently respectable characters from Haverfordwest apparently escaped prosecution within the borough only to end up as "vagabonds in London" in 1356,[39] but we cannot say how such flights were socially perceived. Conversely, such offences as did occur could, by the same token, be blamed on troublemakers from elsewhere: crime in Tenby was being blamed as early as 1528 on an influx of Irish, a trope we shall see becoming familiar in later times.[40] Having examined the records of Marcher lordships, Rhys Davies, though he did find evidence of some gang activities, such as that by William Solers in Clifford in the 1380s, and of some idealized portrayals of the medieval Welsh outlaw, nonetheless concludes that the March was no "criminals' paradise".[41] He notes the enforcement of process by lords and an early predilection for the practice of "binding over to keep the peace", even before this became a favoured tool of royal policy in the fifteenth century.[42] This is an interesting observation. Rather than the simple minor penalty which it later becomes, the bind-over seeks to bring a person who has shown himself to be acting outside the law (or perhaps outside this particular body of law) within its ambit in future. This is an interesting reflection upon attitudes, both popular and "official", towards disorder, for it is predicated on a future submission to authority rather than a present injury to the person or property of the offender.

The fifteenth century saw a sharpening of focus upon crime and criminality within Wales from outside its borders. The revolt of Owain Glyn Dŵr, which, fuelled by prophecy and rooted in Welsh national sentiment and poverty as well as in English royal politics, broke out in September 1400 had a significant impact. Those implicated in the revolt, the disorder of which gradually dissipated over a considerable period of time, were punished. Individuals were executed or imprisoned (locally or in London), more, including whole communities, were pardoned after punitive fines. But the legal implications of the revolt went wider than the individual cases. The anti-Welsh ordinances and statutes which followed from as early as 1401, though they had precursors particularly within the earlier-established English boroughs, made concrete both an ethnic division and the methodology and potency of its expression. Whilst more extreme proposals, such as the imposition of communal kindred liability for breach of the peace (an interesting attempt to combine a traditional compensatory principle with a public order motive) or the wholesale imposition of English criminal law, were not enacted, and some of the measures which were remained imperfectly implemented; the control of the Welsh remained an issue to be revisited in times of tension in the future.[43] Disqualification measures of 1402, preventing the Welsh from holding office, were echoed in 1431 and all measures against the Welsh ratified in 1447.[44] As to specific measures relating to Welsh law itself, a statute of 1413 disallowed rebels and their families from using traditional procedures to recover compensation for injuries suffered in the revolt, a measure which might have seemed obvious to the English but which would be far less so to the kindred of a Welshman killed within a Welsh jurisdiction.[45] Their sentiments might have been more along the lines of the poet Dafydd ap Edmwnd, who complained in the second half of the fifteenth century that the harpist Siôn Eos had been hanged by the "law of London" rather than dealt with by the "law of Hywel".[46] The other danger addressed by statute, to which we have adverted earlier, was the difficulty of the permeability of borders to wrongdoers but not to legal process. The practice of "disclaimer", i.e. claiming that the authority in whose jurisdiction an offender was taken had no authority to put him on trial, was forbidden in 1407, and in 1447 specific provisions for Herefordshire permitted pursuit across the border.[47] Whilst mindful of the danger, adverted to by Davies, of accepting all the claims of disorder in Wales at face value, E.A. Rees has nonetheless argued that there was significant banditry in the country in the fifteenth century and beyond. Not the least interesting of the evidence adduced is from the late fourteenth- and early fifteenth-century poem which contains an account of an annual cycle of criminality, the sort of analysis which was to so excite the early criminologist-statisticians of the nineteenth century.[48]

In the end the details of the legislation provoked by the Glyn Dŵr revolt matter less than the reconfiguration of the relations between Wales and England, particularly in relation to law, which they usher in. In an age of increasing uniformity in England, when the "Common Law" was ceasing to be an expression which simply recognized a lack of geographical limitation to one specific body of rules within England and was entering a phase from which it was to emerge as a complex signifier of national pride and good-old right, the variety of Welsh practice could only seem anomalous. Similarly the surviving customs of the Welsh which had employed a model of compensation to settle disputes could be portrayed, as it had been by Archbishop Pecham as early as the thirteenth century, as a failure to take crime seriously and moreover as a willingness to sell justice for gain. By the end of the fifteenth century, intervention could be more comprehensive, although even then we must not overestimate the force of government will: royal court sessions in remote West Wales were apparently being "compounded", bought off for money, even as the complaints of lawlessness were being made.[49] In 1471 Edward IV appointed his son as Prince of Wales and created a council to assist him, which in 1476 was given authority to hear criminal cases in the Principality, Marches and the English border counties. The Council of Wales and the Marches was revived by Henry VII and a criminal jurisdiction renewed. It settled in Ludlow, a border town.[50]

Notes

1 See S.E. Roberts, *The Legal Triads of Medieval Wales* (Cardiff: University of Wales Press, 2007) p. 357.

2 For the laws in general and their context, see T. Charles-Edwards, *The Welsh Laws* (Cardiff: University of Wales Press, 1989), D. Jenkins, *Hywel Dda: The Law* (Llandysul: Gomer Press, 1986) Introduction, T.G. Watkin, *The Legal History of Wales* (2nd edn, Cardiff: University of Wales Press, 2012) Ch. 4. The website www. cyfraith-hywel.org.uk brings a host of information together. More specific references and particular sources will appear in the notes which follow. The three general textual traditions are known as the *Cyfnerth* (associated with South-East Wales), the *Iorwerth* (with the north) and the *Blegywryd* (with the south-west). For a discussion of the methodologies of blending tradition and innovation within the texts, see R.C. Stacey, *The Road to Judgment: From Custom to Court in Medieval Ireland and Wales* (Philadelphia: University of Pennsylvania Press, 1994) Ch. 7, and for relative antiquity and English influence in relation to parts of the text, see T. Charles-Edwards, *Wales and the Britons 350–1064* (Oxford: Oxford University Press, 2013) pp. 267–273.

3 See Harding and Ireland, *Punishment*, pp. 128–135 for the theoretical analysis.

4 See T. Charles-Edwards, "The *Galanas* tractate in Iorwerth: texts and legal development" in T. Charles-Edwards and P. Russell (eds) *Tair Colofn Cyfraith/The Three Columns of Law in Medieval Wales: Homicide, Theft and Fire* (Bangor: The Welsh Legal History Society, 2005) p. 92.

5 I take this formulation from G. Halsall, *Violence and Society in the Early Medieval West* (Woodbridge: Boydell Press, 1998); see the Introduction. This is not to say that feuding could not in reality become an extended process, only that it need not. For an analysis detailing a feud extending over 60 years, see R. Fletcher, *Bloodfeud: Murder and Revenge in Anglo-Saxon England* (Oxford: Oxford University Press, 2003).

6 See Harding and Ireland, *Punishment*, p. 130 and, on *sarhaed*, Watkin, *Legal History*, p. 54.

7 Charles-Edwards, *Welsh Laws*, pp. 1–5. For an interesting discussion of the nature of early legal systems, see R. F. Green, *A Crisis of Truth: Literature and Law in Ricardian England* (Philadelphia: University of Pennsylvania Press, 2002) esp. Ch. 3.

8 See Jenkins, *Law*, p. 143.

9 See Charles-Edwards, *Welsh Laws*, p. 77.

10 Jenkins, *The Law*, pp. 154–155. See also D.B. Walters, "Honour and shame" in N. Cox and T.G. Watkin (eds) *Canmlwyddiant, Cyfraith a Chymreictod* (Bangor: The Welsh Legal History Society, 2013) p. 229. For the relationship between honour, violence and the face, see V. Groebner, *Defaced: The Visual Culture of Violence in the Late Middle Ages* (P. Selwyn trans., New York: MIT Press, 2004) Ch. 3.

11 See the "Life of St Cadog" in S. Baring-Gould and J. Fisher (eds) *The Lives of the British Saints* (London: Honourable Society of Cymmrodorion, 1907–1913) vol. 2, p. 29. Cadog had given sanctuary for 7 years to the killers.

12 See Jenkins, *The Law*, p. 146, Jenkins, "Crime and tort" p. 4, H. Pryce, *Native Law and the Church in Medieval Wales* (Oxford: Oxford University Press, 1993) p. 142. For secret homicide more generally, see R.W. Ireland, "Medicine, necromancy and the law: aspects of medieval poisoning" *Cambrian Law Review* (1987) 18: 52–61.

13 The discussion within this paragraph and the examples cited are based on W. Davies, *Wales in the Early Middle Ages* (Leicester: Leicester University Press, 1982) Ch. 5.

14 For discussion of this movement in relation to *galanas*, see Pryce, *Native Law*, pp. 78–79, 139–140 and, for later exemplification, Ll. Beverley Smith, "A contribution to the history of *galanas* in late-medieval Wales" *Studia Celtica* (2009) xliii: 87.

15 For the texts, see T. Charles-Edwards, "The Welsh law of theft: Iorwerth versus the rest" in T. Charles-Edwards and P. Russell (eds) *Tair Colofn* (Bangor: The Welsh Legal History Society, 2005) p. 108, and in particular p. 129.

16 See R.W. Ireland, "Law in action, law in books: the practicality of medieval theft law" *Continuity and Change* (2002) 17: 309.

17 And can accordingly give rise to an offence of "thievish arson", see Jenkins, "Crime and tort" p. 3. Similarly a distinction is drawn between theft in this sense and taking which is not denied, *anghyfarch*, for which, and other, classifications, see Jenkins, *Laws*, p. 166. For the law of arson see M. Owen, "*Tân*: The Welsh law of arson and negligent burning" in T. Charles-Edwards and P. Russell (eds) *Tair Colofn* (Bangor: The Welsh Legal History Society, 2005) p. 131.

18 Ibid.

19 For the statute as a whole, see Ll. Beverly Smith, "The Statute of Wales 1284" *Welsh History Review* (1980–1981) 10: 127, Watkin, *Legal History*, pp. 106–112.

20 "In every way your customs seem to be a travesty of justice, as you fail to condemn homicides and many other crimes formally and specifically", Pecham to Llewelyn, as quoted in R. Davies, "The survival of the bloodfeud in medieval Wales" *History* (1969) 54: 338 at 339; and see Pryce, *Native Law*, p. 71.

21 R. Davies, *Lordship and Society in the March of Wales 1282–1400* (Oxford: Oxford University Press, 1978) p. 162.

22 Ibid., p. 32.

23 There is a very interesting example of a pardon for rape in the lordship of Dyffryn Clwyd from 1358, the condition of which is that the defendant work as the lord's mason for 4 years at 12d per week. The only (clearly old) reference I have for this case is PRO SC2/218/7 m.5v; this was passed to me by Shane Kilcommins.

24 See the analysis of the case of John ap Ieuan Goch Saer in 1430 in Smith, "History of *galanas*". See also the wider discussion in R. Davies, "The survival of the bloodfeud".

25 See L. Johnson, "Attitudes towards spousal violence in medieval Wales", *Welsh History Review*, 24 (2009): 81. For native law relating to women, and more generally in respect of *sarhaed* and *galanas*, see M. Owen, "Shame and Reparation: Womens' Place in the Kin" in D. Jenkins and M. Owen (eds) *The Welsh Law Of Women* (Cardiff: University of Wales Press, 1980) p. 40.

26 6/8d was paid for a jury in a theft case in Dyffryn Clwyd in 1332. See Davies, *Lordship and Society*, pp. 160–161 and 170. For the role of the oath in Welsh law, see Pryce, *Native Law*, Ch. 3.

27 For the evidence of the "cucking" (later often "ducking") stool or the wand pillory see R.A. Roberts (ed.), *The Court Rolls of the Lordship of Ruthin or Dyffryn-Clwyd of the Reign of King Edward I* (London: Nabu Press, 1893) pp. 15, 22, 40.

28 The case is fully, and brilliantly, discussed in R. Bartlett, *The Hanged Man* (Princeton, NJ: Princeton University Press, 2004); the quote is at p. 35.

29 See the complaints of Rhys ap Maredudd of Dinefwr against Robert de Tibetot, Justiciar of South Wales for "wrongly compelling Rhys and his Welshmen to plead according to English law", ibid., p. 77.

30 M. Bloch, *Feudal Society* (L. Manyon trans, London: University of Chicago Press, 1965) vol. 1, p. 87.

31 See Pryce, *Native Law*, Ch. 3. For the folk survival, see infra p. 49.

32 See T. Lloyd, J. Orbach and R. Scourfield, *The Buildings of Wales: Carmarthenshire and Ceredigion* (New Haven, CT: Yale University Press, 2006) p. 502. The death is recorded (with a teasing uncertainty) as "propter predam Sancti David".

33 See Pryce, *Native Law*, Chs 6 and 7. It is perhaps worth noting here, in view of the importance of religious division in later years, that Lollardy seems to have had little impact in fourteenth-century Wales; see J. Davies, *A History of Wales* (London: Penguin, 1993) p. 193.

34 For this, see L.K. Little, "Spiritual sanctions in Wales" in R. Blumenfeld-Kosinski and T. Szell (eds) *Images of Sainthood in Medieval Europe* (Ithaca, NY: Cornell University Press, 1991) p. 67, though note that the author here argues for an English or Norman rather than a domestic origin for the practice. This seems unlikely: cursing was a part even of formal legal process in early Britain; see G. Markus, *Adomnán's "Law of the Innocents"* (Kilmartin: Kilmartin House Trust, 2008) p. 15 for a seventh-century instance. For an early Welsh example, see Charles-Edwards, *Wales and the Britons*, p. 247.

35 See S. Dimmock, "Social conflict in Welsh towns *c.* 1280–1530" in H. Fulton (ed.) *Urban Culture in Medieval Wales* (Cardiff: University of Wales Press, 2012) p. 117 at p. 128.

36 See N.W. Patterson, "Honour and shame in Welsh society: a study of the role of burlesque in the Welsh laws" *Studia Celtica* (1981) xvi: 73.

37 In the *Descriptio Kambriae*, II.7. See H. Pryce, "Gerald of Wales, Gildas and the *Descriptio Kambriae*" in F. Edmonds and P. Russell (eds) *Tome: Studies in Medieval Celtic History and Law* (Woodbridge: Boydell Press, 2011) p. 115 at pp. 121–122.

38 26 Henry VIII c.vi (1534).

39 For Summerson on, see *Proceedings of the British Academy*, 89: 115. Dimmock, "Social conflict" p. 121.

40 Ibid., at p. 125.

41 Davies, *Lordship and Society*, p. 170, Davies, *History of Wales*, p. 207.

42 Ibid., p. 172.

43 For a comprehensive and inspired analysis of the revolt and its consequences see R.R. Davies, *The Revolt of Owain Glyn Dŵr* (Oxford: Oxford University Press, 1997), in particular for the measures discussed here pp. 281–292 and Ch. 11.

44 See 4. H.IV c. 32, 9 H.VI c.3, 25 H.VI c.1. For repeals, see 21 Jac.i c.28 s.11.

45 I H.VI c.6.

46 E.A. Rees, *Welsh Outlaws and Bandits: Political Rebellion and Lawlessness in Wales, 1400–1603* (Birmingham: Caterwen Press, 2001) p. 59.

47 9 H.IV c.4, 23 H.VII c.4.

48 Rees, *Welsh Outlaws and Bandits*, passim. For the poem, see p. 99.

49 Ibid., p. 53.

50 See Watkin, *Legal History*, pp. 119–121 for the details.

2 The early modern period
Assimilation and difference

The perceived lawlessness of the Marches of Wales long continued to be a source of complaint. That there was criminality is apparent, but to what extent, if at all, it was greater than in areas, particularly perhaps the remoter ones, of England is impossible to determine. Even if figures were available for comparison it would remain the fact that Welsh lawlessness may have been highlighted as a problem, and therefore more readily discovered, because it was looked for. To what extent the anomalous position of the variant lordships encouraged criminality and to what extent attention was focussed upon criminality because of the anomalous position of variant lordships cannot be known. Davies's wise observation that:

> in no generation has political outrage been unduly inhibited by close attention to the facts; and there is no doubt that the alleged practices of the Welsh March ... were deeply puzzling and offensive to minds habituated to the apparently tidy and uniform procedures of English criminal law.[1]

though written in respect of the fifteenth century, seems equally applicable to the sixteenth. Certainly complaints about disorder in Wales and attempts to combat it were commonplace under the Tudors (who, of course, had reason to understand that threats to established order might come out of the west). It is not my contention that these were simply part of a propaganda campaign with a more far-reaching purpose, but merely to recognize that, throughout time, and up until the present, the spectre of rampant criminality is rarely raised, as Davies suggests, simply as the reporting of a sociological truth.

The solution ultimately favoured, namely the abolition of the rights and privileges of the Marcher lordships, many of which were by then in royal hands, and the assimilation of the law and procedure used within Wales to that of England, will be considered below, but the initial drive to suppress criminality employed an existing institution. The Council of Wales and the Marches, revived yet again in 1525, was reinvigorated in 1534 with the appointment of a new Lord President, Rowland Lee, who had strong views both on the lack of law and order within the jurisdiction of the Council (and indeed within Wales generally) and on the value of a strong deterrent policy in addressing it. Although he was, like his predecessors in title on the Council, a bishop (despite being described by a contemporary as "a mole and enemy of all godly learning"[2]) he, benefitting from the flexibility which the newly nationalized English church afforded him, was relieved of the inability to pass sentence of death which had marked his predecessors. Indeed he proved rather an enthusiast for the rope, although the total of 5,000 executions in 6 years attributed to him by another contemporary, Elis Gruffydd, seems hard to believe.[3] Wrongdoers, including those higher up the social strata, were pursued and deficiencies in the system addressed. "What is the purpose of catching thieves without a place to keep them?" he asked in 1534 after noting the escape of eight offenders from Radnor castle in a year.[4]

If a drive on disorder on the ground was the initial response of Henry VIII's government to the problem of Wales, a more concerted statutory attack followed on the perceived abuses of Welsh lordship, eventually culminating in the eradication of the jurisdictional anomalies within the March. The problems specifically identified were, *inter alia*, of packed juries,[5] of difficulties in pursuit of felons across borders (which apparently included nocturnal ferry crossings from south-west England[6]) and the granting of protection to malefactors by lords, the old Welsh process of *arddel*,[7] which simultaneously exempted criminals from trials in other courts and added to the unsavoury nature of the lord's retinue. Justices of the Peace and of Gaol Delivery were designated to operate within Wales in 1535, albeit that the relative poverty of the localities argued against setting a property qualification. The result was that the system of Quarter Sessions and of Justices operating outside those Sessions, familiar and fundamental elements of the English system of criminal justice, could develop. The Quarter Sessions handled, amongst its other local governmental duties, crime of intermediate gravity, whilst Justices acting singly or in concert would dispose of lesser offences and conduct preliminary investigations into others. It is a system with which we will become familiar in the remainder of this book.[8] Eventually, in the statutes which we term the Acts of Union (of 1536 and 1543), the laws of England and Wales were declared to be the same and the county structure was imposed where lordship had previously held sway. English was to be the language of the law.[9] These were momentous changes and marked the culmination of the policy of assimilation.

Yet the provision of new superior courts, to deal with the most serious crime as well as with civil litigation, together with the continued operation of the Council in Wales and the Marches, should alert us to the fact that it is much too early to assume that a book specifically relating to criminal justice in Wales should end at the reign of Henry VIII. The 1543 statute addressed the legal system within Wales and contains much of interest to the historian of crime. The position of the Council and the responsibilities of the new Justices of the Peace were both consolidated and a superior court, the Great Sessions, originally established by ordinances in 1541, was provided for by the statute.[10] The jurisdiction of the latter was to include "all Treasons, Murders, Felonies, Riots, Routs, unlawful Assemblies, Extortions, Embraceries, Maintenances, Retainers, Concealments, Contempts, and all other Offences and evil Deeds, of what Natures, Names and Qualities soever they be" within their commissions, in accordance with English law and in a similar manner to the superior courts of common law.[11] The Great Sessions were to be held twice each year and were allocated to four circuits, each comprising three Welsh counties (Monmouthshire being assigned somewhat bizarrely to the Oxford Assize Circuit).[12] Provision was made also for the appointment of Chief Constables to keep the peace within the hundreds which had been established. These hundreds were administrative units smaller than the counties and were again long established in English practice. Gaols were to be held by the Sheriffs "within some convenient Place of the Castles of the Shire-towns".[13] Quite apart from the general requirement that English law should be employed, two sections of the Act specifically address the Welsh practice of compounding for serious wrongs by monetary payment. Section 84 states "That from henceforth no manner of Person or Persons, for Murder or for Felony shall be put to his Fine, but suffer according to the Laws of the Realm of England, except it please the King's Majesty to pardon him or them", which seems addressed to the previous practice of payments to lords. Section 125 forbids agreements or attempts to compromise actions (unless approved by the Council or Justices) by all parties concerned, thereby acknowledging the communal rather than individual element of the process, on pain of imprisonment or fine. Not only was the English model of prosecution and trial to be adopted, but the traditional Welsh practice of compensation for wrong was to be expressly outlawed.

Whilst the intention was to assimilate Welsh practice to that in England, the paradoxical effect of the union legislation was to create, through the role assigned to the superior courts of the Council in the Marches and Great Sessions, a role which was embedded within the settlement, a distinct legal entity. Yet, even as the overall legal structure of post-Union Wales is examined, we must remember the observations on the complex of meanings which inhere in the idea of the *extent* of state power which informed the discussion of the Introduction to this book. Taking stock, we may see that the Tudor reforms had formally resolved, even while inscribing a degree of difference in the institutions on either side of a boundary line, the question of the extent of the state in its *geographical* dimension. It had also, both in its express prohibition of "all sinister customs and usages of the Welsh" and implicitly in its suppression of the variety of previous jurisdictional boundaries, resolved the issue of the mechanics of dispute resolution. No role remained for such of the older practices as compensation to the individual or the kin, rather than punishment by constituted legal authority. To this extent, too, the *capacity* dimension of state was settled: the ability, that is, of a unified central system to provide tribunals and enforcement mechanisms capable of imposing general legal principles, at least in theory. But what of the third problematic of state intervention, the penetration of power downwards into the social body? To what extent was the new legal order accepted and how far were older practices and procedures superseded? More broadly we might also ask whether the Tudor settlement reduced or eliminated the problems of law and order which were, or were perceived to be or portrayed as being, such a problem in early modern Wales. The very fact that it is necessary to remind the reader here of the difficulty of distinguishing "fact" from perception should warn us again that we are hostages of our surviving records. Although, as we will see, court records become fuller as time goes on (one of the important by-products of increased state intervention is improved bureaucracy) and provide much important detail, yet records of courts disclose only the later stages of a complex process of social interaction and decision-making. Outside of these, in the absence of sound, comparable statistical data, we are obliged to rely on the anecdotal, with all the problems that such evidence implies. Contemporary commentators in compiling their reports may have personal motives for portraying their environment in a particular way: events may be recorded because they are typical or because they are atypical, because they happen more than they used to or because, though they happened as frequently or less so than they did, they are more noticeable to a changed sensibility. We may not be sure which of these conditions applies. To be aware of the difficulties of our evidence, however, does not mean that there is no point in examining it. To this task we must now turn.

Rowland Lee had warned before the establishment of the Justices of the Peace that the Welsh gentry, upon whom the system would depend, were not up to the task: "there is some bearing of thieves by gentlemen, if this statute go forward, you will have no other but bearing and little justice".[14] That some involved in peacekeeping were corrupt is no doubt true. John Wyn ap Huw, who served as a Justice of the Peace, High Sheriff and Member of Parliament in Caernarfonshire, was accused in 1569 of running a piracy operation based around Ynys Enlli (Bardsey Island) and of influencing members of a Grand Jury ("being his friends and tenants") not to indict one of his gang.[15] A complaint from Cardiganshire which reached the Star Chamber in 1599 alleged embezzlement of munitions and money by members of the local gentry who were Justices of the Peace and Deputy Lieutenants and who, it was claimed, "make their said offices means of great riches to themselves".[16] But there were functional difficulties as well as those relating to the quality of the individual officers in the new system of peacekeeping and, as we will see, they were to persist for a considerable period of time. The geography of Wales, with its scattered population and, away from the coast, problems of communication, meant that even the most assiduous Justices and constables would struggle to maintain order over the country as a whole.[17] The "*lladron yr elltyd*", the "mountain thieves", continued to operate in remote districts in the sixteenth century as they had in the fifteenth.[18] Traditional affinities remained strong, and familiar concerns were voiced over "retainers of gentleman whom they must after the manner of the country bear out in all actions be they never so bad". Specifically, according to Dr David Lewis writing to Sir Francis Walsingham in 1576, such men could be moved out of the way of justice and supported by *cymortha*, a sort of forced levy exacted by these powerful men.[19] The abuse of that old Welsh custom, by men holding offices such as under-sheriff or hundred bailiff in the new political framework, is corroborated by a letter from Richard Price to Lord Burghley, Elizabeth I's Secretary of State, of the previous year.[20] Murray Chapman's investigation of the Great Sessions records in Montgomeryshire amply demonstrates the use and abuse of the legal process by those involved in its administration in the rivalries of great families in the Tudor and Stuart periods. The point remains, however, that the challenge to the effective administration of the new Tudor criminal justice system was threatened not simply by individual venality, but by the topography of the land to which it was applied and the traditional social structures and practices of those who lived there.

One of Dr Lewis's complaints about the abuse of the levy of money deserves a little more consideration. Once the retainers have been moved so as to escape the reach of the law, he says, "the gentlemen will practice an agreement with the parties grieved and then, because the loiterers [i.e. the retainers] have nothing of their own, the gentlemen must help them to a *cymortha* to satisfy the parties damnified".[21] Earlier in this letter the wrongs specified included theft and homicide. The conclusion seems clear: the old Welsh custom of compensation for wrong was continuing even in cases of serious crime a generation after that practice was supposed to have ended. Other sources make clear that indeed this was the case. Nia Powell's examination of the Great Sessions records from Denbighshire in the 1590s supports both the allegations of the protection of defendants in homicide cases by patrons such as the Salusburys of Lleweni and the use of composition to settle liability for killing.[22] The appearance of a mention of "surrayed" (i.e. sarhaed) in an arbitration from Radnorshire of 1563 is eloquent testimony to the survival of older ideas.[23] The ties of kindred, which we have seen underlying the older system of rules and their enforcement, certainly survived the legislation and might be used on occasion to frustrate it. In 1553 a family comprising a father, his two sons and a daughter, their aunt and niece apparently armed with swords, staves and daggers, set upon a constable.[24] Edward, Lord Zouche voiced his concerns about the malign effect of kindred affinities in 1604 ("what a plague it threatens to the country where such vipers are harboured").[25] Other extra-curial means of dispute resolution are also evident; a case of 1592 shows an attempt to use a cleric as arbitrator in a case of theft, which seems to imply not only an anticipated financial settlement rather than that prescribed by law, but also highlights the continuing involvement of the church, at least at the level of popular consciousness, in maintaining order in areas which would have been regarded as essentially secular in England.[26]

It is, of course, difficult to establish the extent to which these older processes and normative structures continued to operate in Wales after the Union, although the contention of this book is that such survivals are neither

unusual nor short-lived. Of necessity, however, they tend to be poorly documented (the "compounding" of a felony by financial settlement was grounds
for prosecution in itself), appearing only incidentally in court records or
anecdotally in private letters or reflections. But that such practices did continue need come as no surprise. Early modern Wales was certainly not a
society unmarked by change, but characteristics which supported the older
pattern – rurality, close ties of kindred and lordship, distance from formal
agencies of law and order – remained the norm in many areas of the country.
Yet difficulties inhere in an attempt to see all of Wales as the same in this
period, despite the apparently universal administrative and comprehensive
assumptions of the Tudor settlement. Regional differences and differences
between town and country no doubt existed. Indeed the population themselves
seem not to have seen themselves as undifferentiated in their relationship to
their liability to the processes of law and order. Powell credibly suggests that
the legal system could be used in particular against "outsiders": in one
Denbighshire case an individual was described as "a deceytfull Southwalis
man wch Cuntrey men were desparat and wild fellows".[27]

None of this, of course, is to suggest that formal legal procedures were not
used, or not used at all against "local" offenders, for clearly they were. W.O.
Williams, having analyzed the oldest surviving Quarter Sessions records in
Wales, which date back to the sixteenth century, declares the system to have
been working "remarkably well".[28] J.G. Jones, working on similar records of
a slightly later date, though he concedes that the effectiveness of the legal
system depended on the attitudes of the local officials, nonetheless also concludes on a positive, though qualified, note. "The evidence suggests", he says:

> that much power was vested by the central authorities in the local gentry,
> and that the system was working. That, however, was only part of the
> story, because lower officials often failed to arrest criminals and, even if
> they were apprehended, prevent them from escaping.[29]

If not all of those within the new system were above reproach, it becomes
clear that a reputation for efficiency in public office was valued, at least formally, and became a feature celebrated in traditional Welsh praise poems. So,
in the poems lauding Morus Wynn of Gwydir, who had served as a magistrate, Sheriff and *custos rotulorum*, his wisdom in office and suppression of
criminality received especial mention.[30] Not all of the Welsh gentry wanted to
be seen as deficient in the exercise of their new responsibilities.

The surveys of Williams and Jones relating to the early years of the new
system on a county level reveal a number of points of interest.[31] First the use
of the recognizance as a means of keeping the peace, a practice which we have
already seen was well established even before the new Henrician settlement,
remained an important method of control thereafter. These recognizances
were often taken by Justices acting outside Quarter Sessions. Where afflictive
punishment was imposed, the Caernarfonshire evidence reveals a complete

infrastructure of punishment. The county gaol, the pillory (to the Caernarfon version of which the petty larcenist Margaret ferch ap Ieuan ap David ap Madog of Ffestiniog no doubt had her ear nailed in 1557[32]) and the stocks were operating alongside the established afflictive penalties of hanging and fining. Nonetheless, despite concern about vagrancy, there seems to have been little early enthusiasm in Wales for the innovative, if costly, Elizabethan method of addressing the problem of idleness more generally, the House of Correction. Paupers were apparently sent, however, alongside those convicted of or suspected of criminality to serve in Elizabeth's army in Ireland, vagrants from which country were paradoxically to be viewed as such a problem in later centuries.[33] This was a cheaper and arguably more utilitarian method of addressing the problem than the newly devised institutional one. The earliest Welsh House of Correction seems to have been built in Carmarthen in 1620.[34] It was soon joined by others, in Ruthin, in Brecon and elsewhere.[35] By that time seeds of a penal revolution which will be considered in later chapters were beginning to grow.

If the Tudor concern with vagrancy, if not the novel English response to it, was taken up in Wales, so too was the issue which Henry VIII's reign had done such work in creating, religious division. It is not necessary here to list the various statutes which sought to impose religious uniformity, but our early Caernarfonshire evidence shows that action was taken within the sixteenth century, albeit perhaps without any particular zeal, against Catholics in the north. The numbers of recusants in South-West Wales seems to have increased as a result of movement of old believers over the English border.[36] To this issue of conformity we will return shortly, but perhaps a consideration of a couple of individual cases on related matters may be worthy of note. The first is that extreme deviation from religious orthodoxy, or even the retention of an ancient belief system, could be stigmatized as witchcraft. As Richard Suggett's admirable survey makes clear, prosecutions for witchcraft are fewer and later than in England, but the first execution for the offence, of the Flintshire healer Gwen ferch Ellis dates from 1594.[37] Suggett's analysis of the period 1568–1699 in Wales reveals only 34 prosecutions for witchcraft, with only 8 guilty verdicts, of which 5 received capital sentences.[38] Yet he also provides a picture of a world in which divination, cursing (including the practice of the suggestively named *galanastra* – "leaving a death" on someone[39]) and magic were common, and resort to "cunning men" routine. Such methods were used, inter alia, to identify thieves and to recover stolen goods. In one case from 1611 a letter from such a "cunning man" was produced in court purporting to show that the defendant was not guilty.[40]

Yet communal sentiment and popular opinion were not, of course, univocal in the early modern period, and differences over fundamental matters were of continuing interest to the law. Variation in religious belief within the seventeenth century as well as in the sixteenth was the cause of many prosecutions. Religion and grand-scale politics continued to be closely intertwined, and outbreaks of public disorder and prosecutions for sedition, even treason, in

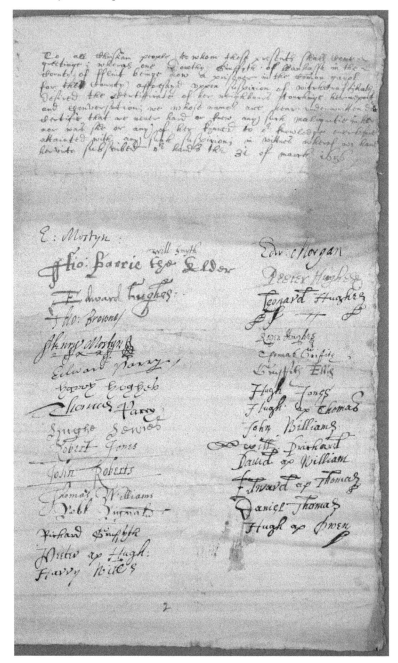

Figure 2.1 Criminality and innocence were matters of communal, not individual, concern. Thirty-one neighbours signed this petition in support of Dorothy Griffin, accused of witchcraft in Flintshire in 1656. It is preserved in the Gaol Files of the Court of Great Sessions.
By permission of Llyfrgell Genedlaethol Cymru/National Library of Wales.

addition to more specific offences against religious observance, should be read in that light at this period. This is not the place to treat such a massive subject in detail, but a couple of general points may be made.[41] First the religious composition of Wales, as has been suggested above, varied from area to area, and so, it seems fair to assume, did the zeal with which dissenters, both Catholic and Nonconformist, were pursued. The second is to note that, despite this element of localism, the Welsh experience and the response were no longer ones which were determined entirely by matters within Wales; the consequences of great events within the "unified" jurisdiction as a whole were played out in Welsh court-rooms. So, for example, under the Commonwealth Major-General Berry was charged with restoring public order, suppressing "immoralities" such as horse-racing and drama, and supervising the activities of the Justices throughout Wales.[42] The Revolution of 1689 had repercussions for the criminal justice system as diverse as anti-Catholic rioting in Welshpool,[43] yet an apparent resistance to the reformulation of the concept of sedition in Denbighshire.[44] It also led to the abolition of the Council of the Principality and the Marches in Wales, the demise of which both marked and contributed to the incorporation of Welsh experience into a greater British polity. To this we must return in due course.

We have got ahead of ourselves, both chronologically and thematically. It is clear from the discussion that religious matters and the safety of the state were closely connected, and matters touching the latter alone were also subject to particular concern. In 1590 Elizabeth Bedo of Criggion, Montgomeryshire, was sentenced to be whipped after declaring that "there was a new king made of the realm of England". The case is of interest because it demonstrates the limits of an apparent flexibility in the legal system. Bedo's earlier offences such as theft and harbouring thieves had been overlooked, "her great age deserving some favour and her fair words promising amendment", but such generosity was not to be extended in the present case, it being "intolerable in a commonwealth that base people of her sort should babble of such high states".[45] The Bedo case reminds us, should we need the reminder, of the discretionary element which is a necessary concomitant of, rather than a simple failure of, all criminal justice systems. Certainly that element was well established within the English system at the time of the Acts of Union. We need to consider the operation of this discretionary system more generally within sixteenth- and seventeenth-century Wales.

At a time when capital punishment was the prescribed default punishment for felony, devices had come about which allowed convictions to be returned but the offender's life spared. A pardon, often with the proviso that the con-victed offender should fulfil a condition (the origins of the penalty of trans-portation), was one such means. Technically the pardon, as a royal grant, lay outside the gift of the local community or those who acted as its representa-tives, although they might petition for the exercise of mercy before the court.[46] More direct local control is evident in the operation of "jury equity", the process by which juries could manipulate their verdict to address not only the narrow issue of guilt or innocence but also the question of how much, if any, punishment the offender deserved. In the typical case the jury would, deliberately and with the acquiescence of the judge, use their role in valuing stolen goods to ensure that a conviction should be for non-capital petty larceny rather than for the capital offence which the true value of the crime would merit. Such a practice had been long familiar in England, where it is almost as old as the jury itself. It is no surprise to learn that Powell finds many examples of it in the records of the Great Sessions relating to Denbighshire in the 1590s.[47] What is surprising, as we will see, is for quite how long the Welsh jury retained its "independence", often in the face of criticism from those in England who had witnessed a gradual retreat from the tradition.[48] Such criticism was not often evident within the early modern period, for it was regarded as integral to the very operation of the jury system. There were complaints about the operation of the jury, but these were of more obvious abuses such as packing it with partial individuals, or, in one case, a jury foreman taking advantage of his position to indict his opponent in an ongoing case.[49] Yet some decisions remain rather mysterious to the modern reader. Whether partiality or credulity was at fault for the wrongful capital conviction for arson of John Griffith John by a Montgomeryshire jury in 1588 is unknown. The victim claimed that he knew that John was responsible, for "Jesus Christ had wrought perfect knowledge thereof in his heart", whilst his wife testified that "she had received notice and assured knowledge in her sleep in bed".[50] On other occasions juries could be more pragmatic in the execution of their duties. In a case from 1572 the jury insisted on calling the prosecutor into their presence, where he joined a selection of his sheep to determine whether disputed animals, which were also in court, had been stolen from his herd. The evidence, as we will see must have been common practice, was given in Welsh, and the jury's acquittal was considered by the Chief Justice of the Great Sessions to be perverse. He instituted proceedings against the jury before the Council, though the case seems to have been remitted again to Great Sessions. To this case we will return again shortly.[51]

Let us first revisit the practice of jury equity, for if we see it operating in the sixteenth century we have evidence too of its vitality in the seventeenth. Grand juries, whose members tended to come from the more socially elevated section of society, albeit one whose daily life might bring them into close contact with less well-off individuals, were responsible for the formal initiation of trials in cases of serious crime. They might use their discretion not to prosecute in particular cases or for particular offences by endorsing the indictment with "Ignoramus" or, after the abolition of the Latin within the court system by statute of 1731, "No [True] Bill". Petty juries who ultimately determined the question of guilt and some of whose members seem not to have been overburdened by privilege, might, as we have just seen, use their power to acquit entirely, or convict for a lesser offence It is important to understand that both juries might use those powers instrumentally, in other words their decisions might be determined by considerations beyond the dispassionate weighing of evidence. Traditionally the analysis of such decision-making tends to attribute such activity to a broad and largely unexplored notion of "sympathy". And sympathy, in the sense of willingness to exempt offenders from the extreme rigour of a system which sought to compensate for the inefficiency of its detection methods by the severity of its prescribed penalty for those who were caught, certainly seems to have been a significant factor. It comes as no surprise then to read that juries were "strongly inclined to give any benefit of the doubt to defendants" in homicide cases, or that conviction rates were higher in offences eligible for "benefit of the clergy" and therefore not punishable by death. This latter claim was the by then often entirely fictitious assertion by first-time offenders that they were members of the clergy, which was proved by the accused either reading or remembering Psalm 51, the "neck verse": the practice had its origins in the medieval church's claim to exemption from secular jurisdiction. That the proceeds of theft continued to be undervalued by juries (for example, goods worth 14s 4/12d assessed at 10d in a case from 1742) to allow a less grimly certain outcome of a felony trial is also not surprising.[52] It may be, however, as I have suggested was the case in a rather later period,[53] that attribution of all such actions to "sympathy" alone might conceal the complexity of the considerations which could inform the jury's decision-making process. The reputation of the accused more generally, the condition of his or her family and dependents, their utility within the local community and the existence or resort to alternative means of dispute settlement might also come into play in this response. If the prosecution of neighbours was a decision influenced by broader considerations of a social nature, and we have seen in the case of Elizabeth Bedo considered earlier that it was, how much more so was their conviction or even their judicial killing? Juries were ideally placed, indeed expected, to interpose this degree of fine tuning into an apparently crude penal system. They were not alone. We must also be aware that local Justices of the Peace, men who again might choose to stress from local knowledge whether a punishment was merited by an offender rather than an offence, might also be influential not only in lesser cases but also in petitions for mercy after a conviction had been returned in graver ones.[54]

The jurisdictional transfers which were noted above in the case from 1572 in which the sheep appeared in court require a little further discussion. For the post-Union criminal justice system was a hierarchical one. Justices acting outside Quarter Sessions reported into those Sessions which in their turn were inferior to the Great Sessions. The relationship between the Great Sessions and the Council in the Marches and Wales was more complex and, because of the loss of many of the latter's records, is difficult to determine precisely, but the Council seems to have passed cases of ordinary crime to the Sessions, as in the case above, though kept for itself issues relating to public order such as affrays and riots.[55] In 1605, however, the imprisonment of William Witherley by the Council in the previous year provoked a significant debate concerning jurisdiction in a wider and more fundamental sense. Witherley applied to the English Court of King's Bench for a writ of *habeas corpus* to determine the legality of his incarceration, but that court's various orders were ignored. Eventually the English judiciary confirmed that *habeas corpus* jurisdiction of the King's Bench extended into Wales, fining and imprisoning the Council's gaoler, Francis Hunnyngs, to demonstrate the point.[56] The case did not, however, conclude the important question of the extent of King's Bench jurisdiction in the neighbouring system and thus of the relationship between the English and Welsh judicial hierarchies, either in civil or in criminal matters. As to the latter, the case of *R v Athoe* of 1723 was important. Athoe, mayor of Tenby in 1721–1722, was indicted for murder along with his son. An application was made by the Attorney General for a writ of *certiorari* (that is to quash ongoing proceedings) to have the trial heard in Herefordshire. Eventually that application was upheld and the Athoes hanged, the Court of King's Bench declaring that:

> it was very difficult to have justice done in Wales, for they are all related to one another, and therefore would rather acquit a criminal than have the scandal that one of their name or relations should be hanged; and that to try a man for murder in Wales was like trying a man in Scotland for high treason, those being crimes not much regarded in their respective places.[57]

The system of post-Union courts was born already attached to the notion of the bureaucratic records of their proceedings and, as stated earlier, such records allow us to explore crime in a quantitative way, counting prosecutions, convictions and punishments before Justices at Quarter Sessions or in Great Sessions. It is axiomatic, however, to all who write about criminal statistics that they be used with caution: as has been pointed out above, the prosecution of crime is the result of a complex series of attitudes and decisions. A crime must be known about, must be considered serious enough to go to trouble and expense to pursue, and a suspect must be discovered and taken before any court process can be initiated. Crucially, too, it must be considered that prosecution is the appropriate means of addressing the crime and settling the dispute. This is a matter on which we have already touched, in the discussion of the case of Elizabeth Bedo. In early modern Wales that decision was based in part upon the availability and suitability of a range of alternatives: self-help, communal direct action, composition (drawing of course on a body of established legal tradition) and arbitration, using neighbours or figures of authority such as clergymen to decide the outcome. We will see all of these methods in operation, but it may be wise at the outset to reflect on the fact that the choice of how to pursue a wrong was not simply that of an atomized individual victim of crime but was made from within a body of social norms and expectations. As Humphreys, writing about Montgomeryshire primarily in the eighteenth century, observes:

> The decision to take a grievance to court had to be weighed against the irreparable damage that could be done to neighbourly life, and, in minor

local cases, where the victim knew the offender as a neighbour, it is quite plausible that a private settlement would be concluded in a majority of instances.[58]

The caution of the concluding remark, with the thrust of which I entirely concur, is, of course, essential: the private and the unofficial often leave few traces for the historian to follow. Yet it would be wrong, even as we recognize the duality, to see public and private justice as stark alternatives, for the latter operated against the backdrop of the former. The threat of prosecution might concentrate the mind wonderfully on the possibility of a compromise.[59]

Our best commentators are aware of such difficulties in discussing prosecution rates without context. Sharon Howard, in a masterly investigation of crime in Denbighshire between 1660 and 1730, interrogates not only the official figures from Great Sessions and Quarter Sessions but also the processes which might lead to a decision to prosecute.[60] Howard finds, perhaps unsurprisingly, that the superior courts were relatively lightly used, in terms of numbers of indictments laid before them, in comparison to those operating in the (possibly atypical) south-east of England whose records have been studied by historians. The type of offence with which the Welsh courts dealt also differed: interpersonal violence featuring strongly, though lethal violence and that featuring the gentry, whose earlier propensity to settle their arguments physically has been observed, declined.[61] Humphreys's study of neighbouring Montgomeryshire between 1690 and 1790 shows violence forming the majority of prosecutions in both Great and Quarter Sessions.[62] Both he and Howard note the susceptibility of local officials, such as constables, bailiffs and excisemen, to violent resistance or the threat of it (although if the evidence is to be believed in the splendidly scatological case in 1682 of William Heighington, who seems to have enforced his authority through flatulence – in one instance he "thundred out his farts that ye men loathed their meate left it and went there ways" – some reaction seems understandable).[63]

Both authors also reveal that property offences made up a relatively limited amount of the business of the upper courts (30 per cent of Great Sessions and 17 per cent of Quarter Sessions indictments in the Denbighshire sample, 28.5 per cent and 15.5 per cent, respectively, in the later Montgomeryshire one).[64] Animal theft, particularly of horses, cattle and sheep, was especially economically damaging and its proceeds, either alive or as meat, easily moved on. Howard finds the trade in stolen livestock to have been as alarming to contemporaries as the theft itself. Open sales and earmarking, both of which precautions go back to the middle ages, sought to protect animals and reputation, whilst advertisement of missing stock, originally orally in public places and later by newspaper could assist pursuit.[65] Howard has found evidence from as early as 1692 of an agreement amongst neighbours to find lost sheep, apparently a precursor of the prosecution associations which were to become common later and an interesting example of shared concern and assumption of responsibility in a local community.[66] Our earlier discussions have shown that ties of kindred and of lordship had survived the Union settlement, but other affiliations based on shared employment or simply geographical proximity remain significant too. They long remain so.

We have seen, in our discussion of the role of Justices and juries that local men (the restriction to men is here intentionally mentioned) controlled, within limits, the operation of the legal process even in relation to court proceedings. Such a finding forces us to confront a spectre which has been looming over the discussion of the post-Union legal system, that of language. The (ungrammatical) section s.17 of 27 Henry VIII c.26 imposes the obligation to "proclayme and keep" court proceedings in English, in which language officers of the law and juries were required to have competence. Yet even English law itself at the time was fully accepting of a system which might use one language for formulae and for record (for which it still used Latin and the "Law French" into which Anglo-Norman had by now degenerated) and another for exchanges within court. Although the preamble to that 1536 Act had condemned the "use of speech nothing like ne consonaunt to the naturall mother tonge used within this realm" to urge an unwarranted difference between Wales and England, it simply cannot have been envisaged that the Welsh language would magically cease to impinge on legal proceedings after the statute. It did not so cease.

We know that evidence was given in Welsh in a case before the Council in 1615 and an interpreter used to translate, though his ability was questioned. The Council in an earlier case had seemed happy to see a Flintshire coroner translate for the benefit of an inquest jury. Before Great Sessions and Quarter Sessions many would have of necessity also been obliged to use their native tongue. Depositions would almost certainly have been routinely translated by local bilingual Justices before trial, a fact which paradoxically explains the rich survival of such material in the records of the Great Sessions. At those trials which took place before them the Justices of the Peace would for the most part have a degree of competence, in many cases an admirable facility, in Welsh. This characteristic can be seen to be in decline from the later seventeenth century, from which time the Welsh gentry became more Anglophile and Anglophone. Such a change can be seen in the use of paid court interpreters from the eighteenth century. Yet Jones has counselled against a too ready acceptance of the contention that the active role of the bilingual Justice of the Peace was by then wholly in abeyance. In relation to jurors then the ability to speak English as prescribed by statute does not necessarily imply any great competence amongst all the members, and certainly not that it was the language of their natural communication. In many instances the statutory condition seems to have been honoured as much in the breach as the observance. The Bangor juryman Thomas Hughes, who had informed his comrades about the proceedings in court in 1742, said that "although he was not master of the English language, so as to understand it readily and clearly, yet he thought he understood it better than the rest of the jury (…many of them understanding none of that language)". In this he was probably exposing a not infrequent state of affairs and one which not only predated his own experience but also survived, as we shall see in the next chapters, well into the nineteenth century.[67]

We must return to matters which have been noted already in the above discussion, for many matters which would satisfy a test of criminality were dealt with without trial. The recognizance remained a regular method of keeping order throughout the seventeenth century and beyond, though as a response to wrongdoing it is frequently overlooked by historians. Gardner's study of late-seventeenth-century Denbighshire reveals that the recognizances could be for comparatively large sums at that period, whilst Howard notes a change in the form of bind-over in the eighteenth century and also a rather earlier decline in the practice of communal (rather than individual) complaints of misdemeanour.[68]

That the legal system in general was becoming rather more formal as time went on is perhaps no surprise. Yet evidence which we have noted in the preceding century as showing that disputes were still being resolved outside it remains robust for the seventeenth. Interesting cases from Montgomeryshire Great Sessions Gaol Files of the mid-seventeenth century allow us glimpses of a world in which (even when unlawful) compensation payments were routinely offered, though the appearance within these records testify that they did not always end the dispute. One case of 1655 has Joan Pova agreeing to offer a year's service with the wages thereof to settle an allegation of theft, subsequently denied, "having nothing to maynteyne her selfe but her worke and Creditt". In a case of rape and robbery from 2 years later the accused's mother-in law apparently returned the stolen purse and told the victim that she "should be Contented for the wronge done her as neighbours should award", indicating a communal element in the setting of the compensation payment.[69]

The communal element remained potent too in the penalties enforced by law: The public theatre of execution and whipping which were mainstays of the formal legal response to criminality in the early-modern period is often regarded as involving simply corporal penalties. Yet the undoubted theatricality of the administration of those measures should remind us that elements of shame and publicity were as important as the physical injury to the offending body. The sentence of the Great Sessions in 1682 that Robert Lewes should wear a sign on his head declaring him to be a sheep thief is (literally) a graphic illustration of those elements. We have, however, noted the erection of Houses of Correction in Wales, a precursor to a newer form of punishment, of the mind rather than the body and reputation, which we will see becoming increasingly dominant in the next chapter.

Let us end here, though, with a major change in jurisdiction which occurred at the end of the seventeenth century as a result of events which had touched the entirety of the British polity. We have noted above that major religious and constitutional issues found their way into Welsh as well as English Court. Such broader concerns ultimately sealed the fate of the Council of the Marches. This body had become identified with the Restoration monarchy and could not survive its overthrow. In particular the Marquis of Worcester, appointed

President in 1672, had removed 27 protestant Justices of the Peace in South Wales in the so-called Exclusion Crisis of 1680, and two influential critics of his perceived crypto-papist actions were heavily fined in an action of *scandalum magnatum* some 3 years later.[70] The statute disbanding the Council explained that:

> the proceedings and Decrees of that Court have by Experience beene found to be an intolerable burthen to the Subject within the said Principality contrary to the great Charter the knowne Laws of the Land and the Birthright of the Subject and the means to introduce an Arbitrary Power and Government.[71]

The abolition of a superior court peculiar to Wales seems a good point at which to reflect upon what has been discovered in this chapter. We have, in contrast to Chapter 1, been able to quote from more cases and to approach on occasions quantitative analyses of crime, for the bureaucratic world of the post-Union world has been more consistently and uniformly generous in revealing their secrets. But the picture which we have seen is one which contains its share of paradox. Wales was assimilated to England in a statutory scheme which simultaneously enshrined its jurisdictional difference. English was to be the language of the law, though it was not always the language of the court. While the legal process drew in Welshmen as Justices and jurors, and while the scope of the criminal code extended to incorporate new concerns such as religious uniformity or vagrancy, there existed still a society in which occult forces were approached to settle disputes, and old practices of offering and accepting compensation for wrong continued with considerable vigour. It is difficult to speak of these latter elements without acknowledging that there were undoubtedly temporal and geographical variations touching such matters, even within the limited period considered in this chapter. Yet the fact that we often discover evidence of such things, and that we discover it within the legal records, should remind us of an important truth. We should not regard the concern with and response to anti-social behaviour and crime within early modern Wales as occupying two different worlds, one "official" and one "unofficial". Both are aspects of, and could be used instrumentally within, the same world.

Notes

1 Davies, *Revolt*, p. 289.
2 See J.G. Jones, *Early Modern Wales, c. 1525–1640* (Basingstoke: Palgrave Macmillon, 1994) pp. 58 *et seq.* for Lee. The quote is from John Vaughan, see p. 59. See also Rees, *Welsh Outlaws*, Ch. 11.
3 Ibid., p. 60.
4 Ibid., p. 62.
5 See 26 H.VIII c.4.
6 See 26 H.VIII c.5, c.6 s.vii.

7 See 26 H.VIII c6 s.v. See also 26 H.VIII c.11 on affrays in border counties and c.12 on benefit of clergy in Wales.

8 27 Henry VIII c.5, though the 1536 statute apparently overtook the process (Watkin, *Legal History*, p. 126). The statutes considered above are brought together in I. Bowen, *The Statutes of Wales* (London: T.F. Unwin, 1908) and are further discussed in Jones, *Early Modern Wales*, Ch. 2.

9 For the Union, see Watkin, *Legal History*, Ch. 7. The principal statutes are 27 H.VIII, c.26 and 34–35 H.VIII, c.11.

10 See J.H. Baker, *An Introduction to English Legal History* (4th edn, London: Oxford University Press, 2002) p. 31. For the Great Sessions in general, see G. Parry, *A Guide to the Records of Great Sessions in Wales* (Aberystwyth: National Library of Wales, 1995) Introduction.

11 34–35 H.VIII, c.11, ss.12, 13.

12 Note Chapman's suggestion that there may have been early attempts to exploit the divisions between the Circuits in a way parallel to the earlier exploitation of lord-ship boundaries, despite the fact that the jurisdiction was uniform. His discussion of the felony jurisdiction in Montgomery (granted in 1562) which effectively removed the borough obligation to report into Great Sessions should remind us that the royal power to grant jurisdictional privileges to particular towns remained unaffected by the settlement. See M. Chapman, "Life in Montgomeryshire during the Tudor and Stuart periods" in *National Library of Wales Journal*, (2011) xxxv, 2: 70 *passim*. pp. 74, 75.

13 Ibid., ss.71, 72.

14 Letter from Lee to Cromwell, 12 March 1536, excerpted in the source documents admirably brought together in J.G. Jones, *Wales and the Tudor State* (Cardiff: University of Wales Press, 1989) p. 169.

15 Ibid., p. 183, the complaint of Morgan ap John to Star Chamber. See also p. 185 for another report of piracy based in Cardiff.

16 *David Lloyd v Richard Price and Morgan Lloyd* in ibid., pp. 194–195. See also J.G. Jones, *Law, Order and Government in Caernarfonshire 1558–1640* (Cardiff: University of Wales Press, 1996) p. 153.

17 See the action of the Council in seeking to suppress alehouses, "many being in desert and secret places" in March 1573, extracted in Jones, *Tudor State*, pp. 188–189. In fact this measure relates specifically to the English border counties, but there is no reason to doubt the existence of a similar underlying problem to the west. Certainly the wildness of the country was no doubt of assistance to the quasi-legendary Tudor robber and trickster Twm Siôn Cati (identified in reality as one Thomas Jones), whose popularity in folk tales can be seen as an interesting inversion of the proclaimed benefits of the newly-imposed system of order.

18 Rees, *Welsh Bandits and Outlaws*, Chs 6, 14.

19 Ibid., p. 200.

20 Ibid., p. 198.

21 Jones, *Tudor State*, p. 200.

22 See N.M.W. Powell, "Crime and the community in Denbighshire during the 1590s: the evidence of the records of the Court of Great Sessions" in J.G. Jones (ed.) *Class, Community and Culture in Tudor Wales* (Cardiff: University of Wales Press, 1989) at p. 261.

23 See R. Suggett, "The Welsh language and the Court of Great Sessions" in G. Jenkins (ed.) *The Welsh Language Before The Industrial Revolution* (Cardiff: University of Wales Press, 1997) p. 153 at p. 165.

24 W.O. Williams, *Calendar of the Caernarvonshire Quarter Sessions Vol 1, 1541–1558* (Caernarfon: Caernarvonshire Historical Society, 1956) pp. lxxix, 124.

25 Jones, *Law, Order and Government*, p. 194.

26 See Powell, "Crime and the community" pp. 267–269.

27 Ibid., p. 270.
28 W.O. Williams, *Calendar*, p. lxxxiv.
29 Jones, *Law, Order and Government*, pp. 167, 178.
30 Ibid., pp. 198–199, though note Jones's view of the differences between the two poems there quoted.
31 See Jones, ibid., Chs V and VI for his discussion; Williams, *Calendar*, Introduction.
32 Williams, *Calendar*, p. 159.
33 Chapman, "Life in Montgomeryshire" pp. 81–83.
34 See T.H. Lewis, "Documents illustrating the County Gaol and House of Correction in Wales" in *Transactions of the Honourable Society of Cymmrodorion, Session 1946–47* (1948) p. 232. The House of Correction statute was of 1597, 39 Eliz c.4; see also 7 Jac.I c.4 (1609).
35 See Lewis, "Documents illustrating the County Gaol", Appendix nos 3 and 9, which latter presupposes a County House of Correction in existence before 1692–1693.
36 See Jones, *Law, Order and Government*, pp. 155–166.
37 R. Suggett, *A History of Magic and Witchcraft in Wales* (Stroud: The History Press, 2008) Chs 1 and 2.
38 See Suggett, *History of Magic*, Ch. 1.
39 Ibid., p. 59 and see Chapman, *Criminal Proceedings*, case no. 16.
40 Suggett, ibid., Ch. 4, and, for the case, p. 80.
41 For religion and society generally at this time, see, e.g., P. Jenkins, *A History of Modern Wales 1536–1990* (London: Routledge, 1992) Part Two. For legal impact, Watkin, *Legal History*, pp. 145–155, J.S. Gardner, "Justices of the peace in Denbighshire, 1660–1699", unpublished Ll.M. thesis (University of Wales, Aberystwyth, 1984) pp. 19–24. For crime in particular localities, ibid., pp. 86–120, S. Howard, *Law and Disorder in Early Modern Wales: Crime and Authority in the Denbighshire Courts, c. 1660–1730* (Cardiff: University of Wales Press, 2008) pp. 154–186.
42 In August 1655; see Watkin, *Legal History*, p. 150.
43 M. Humphreys, *The Crisis of Community: Montgomeryshire, 1680–1815* (Cardiff: University of Wales Press, 1996) p. 228.
44 Howard, *Law and Disorder*, p. 165.
45 Chapman, "Life in Montgomeryshire" pp. 80–81.
46 See Jones, *Law, Order and Governance*, pp. 170–171.
47 Powell, "Crime and the community" p. 288. For the antiquity of the practice in England, see R.W. Ireland, "Theory and practice within the medieval English prison" *The American Journal of Legal History* 56, (1987) xxxi: 64–67.
48 Infra p. 73.
49 See Williams, *Calendar*, p. 218.
50 Chapman, "Life in Montgomeryshire" pp. 76–77.
51 M. Chapman, "A sixteenth-century trial for felony in the Court of Great Sessions for Montgomeryshire" *The Montgomeryshire Collections* (1990) 78: 167 *et seq*.
52 Howard, *Law and Disorder*, pp. 66, 86, 133–140;, Humphreys, *Crisis of Community*, pp. 244–249 for relevant figures and discussion. On jury equity, see also Gardner, "Justices of the peace" p. 76.
53 Ireland, "Putting oneself on whose country? Carmarthenshire juries in the mid-nineteenth century" in T.G. Watkin (ed.) *Legal Wales: Its Past, Its Future* (Cardiff: Welsh Legal History Society, 2001) *passim*.
54 Humphreys, ibid.
55 See Parry, *Great Sessions*, pp. xxii–xxiii.
56 See P. Halliday, *Habeas Corpus: From England to Empire* (Cambridge, MA: Harvard University Press, 2010) pp. 11–14.
57 See 1 *Strange* 553; the passage is quoted in Parry *Great Sessions* p. xvii, and see generally pp. xiv–xxii.
58 Humphreys, *Crisis of Community*, p. 224.

59 See, for example, Suggett, "Welsh language" p. 165.
60 See Howard, *Law and Disorder*, "Investigating responses to theft in early modern Wales: communities thieves and the courts" *Continuity and Change* (2004) 19: 409.
61 *Law and Disorder*, Chs I and II.
62 Humphreys, *Crisis of Community*, p. 225.
63 Howard, *Law and Disorder*, pp. 147–150, cf. Humphreys, *Crisis of Community*, p. 226.
64 Howard, *Law and Disorder*, p. 102, which reveals a significantly lower prosecution rate per head than in south-eastern English studies; Humphreys, *Crisis of Community*, p. 225.
65 For the middle ages, see Ireland, "Law in action" p. 318. For a fascinating discussion of the marking of sheep and its significance, see the depositions taken in a case of theft from 1656, case no. 318 in M. Chapman (ed.), *Criminal Proceedings in the Montgomeryshire Court of Great Sessions: Transcript of Commonwealth Gaol Files 1650–1660* (Aberystwyth: National Library of Wales, 1996). The police might retain registers of sheep earmarks even in the mid-twentieth century, see Ceredigion Archives POL 9/4/16 for a beautiful version and the observations of H.J. Owen, *From Merioneth to Botany Bay* (Dolgellau: Evans, 1952) Ch. XIV.
66 See Howard, *Law and Disorder*, pp. 105, 123.
67 For the cases mentioned here and a discussion more generally, see Suggett, "Welsh language" and J.G. Jones, "The Welsh language and local government: justices of the peace and the Courts of Quarter Sessions *c.* 1536–1800" (Cardiff, 1977), see also in Jenkins (ed.), *The Welsh Language Before the Industrial Revolution*, p. 181.
68 Gardner, "Justices of the peace" p. 65, Howard, *Law and Disorder*, pp. 188–189, 204–205.
69 See Chapman, *Criminal Proceedings*, nos 230, 412, 416. Note also no.1 (1650), where the complainant refused to accept compensation for stolen sheep "feareinge to … smuther up such a Felony". Such refusals and prosecutions might, of course, be tactically rather than ethically determined.
70 See G. Jenkins, *The Foundations of Modern Wales 1642–1780* (Oxford: Oxford University Press, 1993) pp. 164, 143–144.
71 1 Will.&M. c.27.

3 The eighteenth century

Courts, curses and confinement

As our discussion moves into the eighteenth and particularly perhaps the nineteenth centuries we might expect everything to change. We observe the operation in society generally of big things, which have big names: The Enlightenment, The Industrial Revolution. The economy, and with it the demography and topology of Wales changes: extractive industries – coal in the south and north-east, slate in the north-west, lead in the west – and manufacture – wool in the east, tinplate in the south-west – see to that, but also potentially open up fissures between industrial and agricultural areas. More immediately relevant to this narrative are the changes in the legal and penal systems within the period: the abolition of Great Sessions, the increasing ambit of the criminal law and the change in the nature of the criminal trial, the "penal revolution" which sees the dominance of incarceration at the expense of corporal and capital measures, and the pursuit, in the potent phrase of the Webbs, of "the fetish of uniformity" in punishment[1], the development and spread of the "new police". The aim of this and the following chapter is to assess the effects which such changes had upon the operation of the criminal justice system.

One preliminary point may be worth making. In the period to which we now turn, the creation and survival of record evidence (from both official and other sources) continues to allow us, generally speaking, a still fuller access to information than has been the norm so far. Not only that, but the modern digitization of such material as provincial newspaper reports and court records makes the mining of such evidence a more practical operation than once it was. The National Library of Wales has a searchable database of a century of Great Sessions Gaol files, already instructively used by Woodward to analyze patterns of animal theft and burglary, whilst my own database of those remanded for felony in Carmarthenshire between 1844 and 1871 allows a similar opportunity to exploit the detailed outcomes of a heavily bureaucratized Victorian criminal justice system. The point is made here not simply to excuse in advance what may be two chapters rather more detailed than those which have come before, but also, more importantly, to invite the reader to engage directly with the source materials. To read about legal history is, I hope, interesting, but to "do" it is even more so.[2]

Patterns of crime in eighteenth century Wales are, as might be expected, in many ways similar to those found in the last chapter; theft and violence, the "common colds" of social pathology but also the chief concerns of the criminal law, continue to appear frequently in the records. At Quarter Sessions level, the thefts are often opportunistic and are of minor value, Denbighshire records show, for example, the prosecutions of Margaret Davies in 1729 for taking wool from the bodies of sheep and, in 1736 of Katherine Thomas for taking honey from a tree.[3] Related but more serious offences were common at Great Sessions: burglary and housebreaking and the theft of sheep (in their entirety!) seem to have been responsive to seasonal and economic changes, although it is clear that, in particular in relation to animal theft, both of sheep and horses, it would be naïve to ascribe all such offending to desperate and casual opportunists.[4] But many were driven by short-term motives. The petition signed by 98 of the leading citizens of Denbighshire on behalf of the recidivist sheep-stealer Edward John in 1793 who had been sentenced to hang, in drawing attention to the fact that "the said convict having a Wife and children was pressed by extreme want and Poverty to commit the said offence" is testament both to the circumstances of the crime and the continued reluctance of the local community to abandon the issue of justice entirely to the demands of the law.[5] As to the use of violence, then this is, predictably, often associated with alcohol and in some cases is connected to long-running family quarrels; the importance of kindred in Welsh social organization has still, it seems, by no means disappeared.[6] Domestic violence, when prosecuted, seems to have been met generally with bind-overs, the use of which continues to prove a most important means of social control.[7]

Other offences of a kind mentioned previously continue to occupy the courts. Smuggling, and the violent exchanges with officials which often resulted from attempts to suppress it, was common on the coast. It did not always lack an element of wider social support, as the Customs officer who was obliged to fire on an angry crowd in New Quay in self-defence found. He was bound over by the local magistrates to appear at Assize in 1704.[8] Ninety years later, no less than 600lbs of tobacco were removed in raids on warehouses on the North Wales coast.[9] Taking goods from wrecked ships (though tales of deliberate wrecking seem to have been largely apocryphal) and from the bodies washed up on shore was regarded as fair game and customary right, though extreme behaviour such as that practised at the wreck of the *Phoebe and Peggy* at Solva (Pembs) in 1773 or the *Charming Jenny* at Crigyll (Anglesey) was guaranteed to cause official outrage. Two men were sentenced to death, one of them being executed, after a trial in distant Shrewsbury in 1774 relating to the latter case. Local men of importance were implicated in the affair and the magistrates in the area had shown little urgency in addressing the case.[10]

Lewis Morris, himself a Customs official, wrote a poem condemning the Crigyll robbers, but he had more direct contact with disorder involving local squirearchy in relation to his work connected with minerals, in which he represented the Crown Estates.[11] The expansion in extent and value of the Welsh extractive industries in the eighteenth century and the concentration of young men, often from outside the immediate local area, which the development of such industries attracted led to incidents of mass disorder as well as individual crime. Such incidents might have a racial element, of a type hitherto largely concentrated on the tension between the predominantly English boroughs and the Welsh countryside (a tension which might still surface, as it did in a disturbance near Denbigh in 1754).[12] The employment of English miners on the Wrexham coalfield caused disturbance in 1776, and the resentment against the colliers and agents drafted in from Cornwall, Northumbria and Lancashire remained apparent.[13] The same peer-groups, drawn up, as we have seen, increasingly around occupation in addition to more traditional family or lordly ties, who would take to the streets to defend their jobs, could also be seen to be active in other areas of popular disturbance such as the food riots which marked eighteenth-century Wales. It was colliers, for example, who led the Flintshire riots against perceived problems in food supply in 1740, when such disturbances were widespread in Wales as a whole.[14] Interestingly the Flint rioters seem to have retained a sense of affiliation to the local gentry, expressing support for and perhaps being abetted by Sir Thomas Mostyn. Similarly, rampaging Cardiganshire miners in 1731 had been led by a prominent local squire, Thomas Powell of Nanteos.[15] Gentry involvement in popular disorder still existed in the eighteenth century then, but it seems to have been changing in its nature. The gentry are involved, or, more typically as the century passes, are invoked, as representative of particular employment or political interests rather than as capable of mobilizing a band of "retainers" more feudally conceived. Political riots within the eighteenth century (although as we have seen at Flint it is too simplistic to imagine that riots relating to "politics" or "food" or "religion" or "employment" sit comfortably in every case as discrete entities) are notable events, though we should not be seduced into thinking that popular disturbances, now so well explored by Welsh historians, were everyday occurrences. Some of these disturbances seem directly related to events touching political or religious tensions which extend beyond the immediate locality, the "Jacobite" riots in Welshpool for example or the anti-Noncomformist riot in Wrexham,[16] even though local factors are clearly important. The riot in Carmarthen in 1755 seems to have provided a precedent for a continuing tradition of violence in relation to local politics, the competing factions of which still remain inscribed in the street names of the town, which long endured. The Carmarthen borough election as late as 1831 was postponed and could only be held with a large number of policemen drafted into the town, with detachments of troops being held in reserve.[17]

Perhaps the most alarming of the "political" disturbances of the eighteenth century were, however, those which looked beyond the local or even national concerns towards the international arena, in particular to revolutionary France. Rioting in the 1790s involved protests against the food supply and the militia regulations.[18] Though invocation of the French cause in the disturbances was muted (France had, after all, invaded Wales in 1797, and loyalty was publicly exhibited in Aberystwyth and elsewhere by public burnings of *The Rights of Man* or effigies of its author Thomas Paine, both regarded as dangerously radical[19]), it was not unknown. John Griffith, who had threatened thunderstorms should he be arrested, was, despite this evidence of a less than rational appreciation of his own capabilities, tried for sedition at Cardiff in 1800 having praised Bonaparte. He pleaded insanity and received two months' imprisonment. But, for others who rioted at this time, even though the reason seemed entirely domestic, as for the two rioters hanged in Merthyr in 1801, the consequences were severe.[20] The British government was jumpy and was by no means inclined to take risks with popular disturbances. Cases as serious as riot, of course, would be brought in the Court of Great Sessions, whose judges might be relied upon to uphold a Government position rather more vigorously than did local magistrates. The responses of this latter class to instances of popular disorder were guided more frequently by sensitivity to local conditions. Whilst their responses were sometimes severe in the eighteenth century, they were not uniformly so.[21] But the superior judiciary could generally be relied upon to send a less ambiguous message. When Hardinge J used the occasion of a trial of two food rioters at Brecon in 1800 to deliver a piece of fierce anti-French rhetoric the defence of a broader constitutional system was clear,[22] as, more remarkably, was the translation into Welsh of Sir William Ashhurst's patriotic *Charge to the Grand Jury* of Middlesex of 1792.[23] The threat to government which inhered in mass action was by no means to be tolerated by its representatives in Wales.

The French Revolution and the war which followed it had other consequences for the criminal justice system. Soldiers and sailors both in service and discharged contributed to the number of vagrants found in Wales at the turn of the nineteenth century. Large numbers of vagrants, carrying passes, were escorted through the country by parish constables, their journeys often beginning or ending at seaports.[24] But, as we know, vagrancy had been seen as a more general problem long before then. The Master of the House of Correction in Denbighshire claimed expenses for conveying a total of 440 vagrants to Caernarfonshire between 1740 and 1742, many, no doubt, to be returned to Ireland, so often regarded as the source of the problem of the displaced poor.[25] In 1786 the Cardiganshire Bench, alarmed by the arrival in the county of "a numerous and desperate gang of villains" ordered Justices and constables to search their localities at least one night each month for "vagrants, strollers and other suspicious persons". Innkeepers failing to report suspicious persons were to lose their licences and ran the risk of being tried as accomplices. Notices advertising these new measures were to be set up in "the most publick places" in the parishes.[26] Similar concerns about outsiders in neighbouring Carmarthenshire in the 1770s apparently saw that Bench adopting a policy of asking every "Englishman that comes among us" what their business was.[27] It is interesting to see that, whether they came from the west or the east, strangers were still being treated with suspicion, at least within the more homogenous rural Welsh heartlands.

Let us turn from these offences which might be construed as offences against public authority and examine other, more general, offences which troubled eighteenth-century Welsh communities. Whilst presentments of minor wrongs and nuisances could be made in manorial courts and courts leet in a quasi-public capacity, and whilst parish constables, whom we have noted above in Montgomeryshire acting with a degree of organization which belies their stereotyped portrayal, had a role in peacekeeping alongside the Justices, it remained true that the onus lay mostly on individual victims of wrong to respond to it.[28] I have used the general formulation ("respond") deliberately, for as we saw in the last chapter the range of possible responses was wide and was by no means restricted to, or even dominated by, criminal prosecution. Self-help was still an option for those confident enough to try it and might spill over into wider acts of revenge, as seems to be the case when some incidents of damage to property and livestock as well as some assaults which appear in the records are investigated.[29] Such matters, of course, tend to be documented only when they underlie subsequent criminal actions so it is impossible to tell how often they occurred. Perceived wrongs (whether technically criminal or not) against a local moral order rather than those touching a specific complainant might result in concerted action by local communities, or sections thereof, acting in concert. It is not clear with what intent the suspected infanticide Jane Evans was visited and interrogated by a mass of her neighbours in Denbighshire in 1768,[30] but some such visitations at least could be clearly punitive. We have little evidence from the eighteenth century to suggest that the *ceffyl pren* of South West Wales (which we will meet in the next chapter) was active then, but we do know that property belonging to perceived offenders against community norms and even on occasions the individuals themselves were sometimes attacked with stones by aggrieved neighbours.[31] The institution of the mock trial was also current in popular consciousness, showing a positioning of popular penality within the context of, and with a parodic awareness of, the "official" version thereof.[32] Again, however, the clandestine and potentially illegal nature of such popular responses make them resistant to any form of quantitative analysis, although we will see variants continuing to operate within the next century.

Negotiated settlements and compensation agreements may similarly escape documentation, though some of these too do occasionally come to light. A copy of an agreement of November 1752 settling a dispute over a lamb appears in the Merioneth Quarter Sessions records, and not long later the same court refers a dispute to the arbitration by solicitors, with a criminal trial to follow if an agreement could not be reached.[33] Such recognition of extra-curial settlement either as an alternative to or, as in a case of riot and assault from Cardiganshire in 1786, in addition to,[34] a criminal conviction demonstrates eloquently the fluidity of the justice system in practice and the lack of clear distinctions between civil and criminal, punitive and compensatory remedies drawn by those involved. In a tendency which echoes the medieval invocation of the power of the church as instrumental in dispute settlement, the spread of Nonconformity in Wales also seems to have produced a rise in the use of dispute resolution overseen by the chapel, rather than by the secular power.[35]

All of these responses, whether "formal" or "informal", depended upon the actual or supposed offender being identified. But what about where the wrongdoer's identity was unknown? It is clear that, throughout the eighteenth century and well into the nineteenth, trust continued to be placed in the supernatural to reveal the truth. Resort to "cunning men" seems to have been a not infrequent way of pursuing suspected persons or missing goods, and the knowledge that such powerful figures would be consulted might force a guilty party to reveal himself rather than be exposed.[36] Belief in such things was not the monopoly of the victim. However Robert Darcy, who used astronomy and a pack of cards in his practice, was prosecuted for obtaining money by false pretences by a dissatisfied client, Edward Phillips, in 1740. Other practitioners used a mirror to reveal wrongdoers and forms of "ordeal", using cheese, or a toad baked in a clay ball might be employed to similar ends centuries after the abolition of church-sanctioned versions of such tests had disappeared from the world of the law courts.[37] Even when legal punishment was visited upon these "cunning men", their reputation might still survive. William Griffiths was frequently visited by clients even while confined within Cardiff gaol for "pretending to conjure".[38] Similarly, the law seems to have had limited success in dealing with a related phenomenon, the use of "cursing wells" to invoke punishment on those who had done wrong. These places established themselves in the late eighteenth and nineteenth centuries and existed clearly as a kind of symbolic inversion in purpose of the "holy wells" so widespread in Wales The cursing well might be immensely well used despite official disapproval, particularly the one at Ffynon Elian near Llandrillo, the keeper of which received six months' imprisonment with hard labour for operating it as late as 1831.[39] The persistence and belief in such methods is remarkable and reflects a potent strain in Welsh popular belief which merits our serious consideration. In an age before routine police investigation of offenders, resort to those with access to "sight" might be the only possible hope of a victim in the face of otherwise predictable failure, whilst a curse upon a known wrongdoer could bring satisfaction to that victim without the same cost, financial and social, which might result from prosecution. Whilst the whole looks odd in a country which was increasingly lauded for its religiosity, it relies upon a similar epistemological base. The injustices of the physical world might perhaps be redressed by an appeal to powers outside it.

Yet as newspapers became more common and developed a larger readership, a rather different method of pursuing stolen goods could be exploited. Stolen horses, high-value commodities which could be, and indeed generally had to be, sold on to realize their value, were advertised in newspapers or in specially produced and circulated handbills. This process could indeed lead to successful convictions, as cases of 1757 and 1790 make clear.[40] The problems of meeting the costs of prosecutions or of offering rewards were addressed by an increase in the practice, mentioned in the previous chapter, of forming prosecution associations in which individuals grouped together to share the burden and to indicate a willingness to address the problem of criminality. Such bodies are, of course, also to be found frequently in England, but nonetheless it comes as some surprise to find an agreement by a vestry in 1772 "that we the inhabitants of this parish do hereby jointly agree together to prosecute on all felony that whomsoever will be found within this parish" in so small a community as the Cardiganshire parish of Llanrhystud.[41] Even within the nineteenth century when it might be assumed that the introduction of the "new police" would render such associations redundant they might still be created; Llanfair Caereinion in Montgomeryshire created one as late as 1875.[42] In truth the onus for prosecution of many felonies remained primarily on the victim long after the new constabulary, conceived originally as a preventative rather than an investigatory or persecutory body, was established.

If a prosecution were brought to court, whether upon individual or communal initiative, the question as to the language in which the proceedings were to be conducted continued to be a real one, albeit one which rarely impinged on the wider British legal consciousness. Paradoxically, legal language had become an issue outside Wales in the 1730s when an Act finally made English the only acceptable language of the law at the expense of Latin and "Law French". In opposing the measure, a reactionary Raymond LCJ had raised the spectre of Welsh being used if the abandonment of a tradition of less colloquial forms was allowed. To ensure clarity a second Act maintaining the monopoly of English in proceedings in Wales was required in 1733, the year when the original Act (of 1731) came into force.[43] But, as we have seen earlier, it is easier to produce a statute than to create a new linguistic culture.

Even before a matter came to court the issue of language might become material. Cardiganshire magistrates, mindful of the reality of the language of everyday trade, were circulating printed Welsh versions of statutes concerning weights and measures within the county in 1786.[44] There were also occasions upon which it was urged that the Riot Act, the reading of which had important legal consequences for the powers of the authorities to disperse an assembly, should be promulgated in the language which the crowd was likely to understand, as at disorder in Flintshire in 1730.[45]

Despite the "Anglicanization" of the gentry over time, the evidence suggests that, as we saw in the previous chapter, many of the trials before magistrates alone and many of the preliminaries to trials before higher tribunals still depended upon familiarity with the native tongue.[46] Paid interpreters are also to be found appearing at trial, with an indication of the level of the fees they might expect for their services: Merionethshire Quarter Sessions interpreters at mid-century were receiving sums of 6s/8d or 10s.[47] A visitor describing the "Assizes" [i.e. the Great Sessions] in 1793 remarked that "pleadings are in Welch, explained to the judges, as I was informed, by interpreters". The process was not without its imperfections, as recognized by a commentator in 1803:

> This interpreter, however distinguished may be his skill, can never convey the exact meaning, the tone, the gesture, as it bears upon the verbal impact of the evidence, the confidence or hesitation of the witnesses. The consequence is, that property and even life may be endangered by a defective interpretation.[48]

The position might even be a dangerous one for the interpreter himself, as the one who acted in the proceedings against those accused of the murder of William Powell in 1770 found to his cost when he was fired upon by "a man disguised in an ass's skin". Some of the defendants in this case had to be brought back into court to have the sentence of death translated for them, they apparently not having understood it originally.[49]

The defendant might not be the only one struggling linguistically in a trial. We saw in the last chapter that the jury had a tradition of "independence", a capacity to decide cases and, ultimately, punishments by reference to reasoning which extended beyond the narrow criteria of reference which inhered in the framing of an indictment or the details of the rules of evidence. We know that the return by jurors of "not guilty" verdicts or of "partial" verdicts (i.e. that the defendant was guilty of a lesser offence than that alleged) remain common in England as well as Wales in the eighteenth century. Yet specific aspects need to be considered when Welsh juries are considered. There are cultural factors at work here, not least the fact that jurors might not have sufficient English properly to follow the evidence.

Let us note the phenomenon first, before exploring its possible rationale. Watson's discovery that in Great Sessions the jurors' reluctance to convict women of violent crime was the inverse of their refusal to find guilty verdicts in cases of rape reveals something beyond the specific characterization of women and suggests to her "a distinctively Welsh approach to criminal justice".[50] Both Williams-Jones and Humphreys, in their historical surveys of Merionethshire and Montgomeryshire respectively, remark on the tendency of juries in those counties to find only partial verdicts, the latter finding this to be the case in 15 out of 24 guilty verdicts between 1760 and 1784. A single example, the case of Edward Whittingham in 1742 whose burglary of goods apparently worth 14s 4/12d was valued at 10d by the jury, will suffice to illustrate the nature of the practice.[51] Woodward's study of horse-theft finds that the percentage of "no bills" found by Grand Juries (i.e. the discontinuance of proceedings before trial of issue) and acquittals delivered by petty jurors at trial exceeds the average for similar crime to be found in England.[52] It is, of course, impossible to get behind the inscrutability of the jury's decisions in any case and to determine with confidence how much of their liberality was informed by linguistic factors. It must be repeated that "jury equity" is common enough in eighteenth-century England to mean that language cannot be the only, or even the dominant, motor. Clearly, however, an inability to follow the case in court is liable to result in decisions being based on factors extraneous to the evidence of a kind considered in the previous chapter. Certainly we have evidence that jurors, even at Great Sessions, might indeed struggle with the language of the court, and the case of the Bangor glazier who took it upon himself to act as an interpreter for his fellow jurymen in a case of 1742 was discussed above.[53] It would be naïve in the extreme to assume that this was an isolated instance, as evidence of the continued linguistic disability of jurymen of the nineteenth century, to be considered in the next chapter, will confirm.

Yet, when defendants were convicted, the range of punishments open to the court was changing very significantly in the eighteenth century, and that change is traceable in the records of Welsh courts. Not that all was discontinuity: the extensive "Bloody Code" of capital offences which prevailed in the legal system of England and Wales was not effectively dismantled until the 1830s. In 1819 it was reported that 223 offences were still punishable by death.[54] People continued to be hanged in Wales and on occasion that penalty was exacerbated by those further punishments which were permitted by the law. The gibbet, in which the body of the executed was suspended and left on public display as a continuing process of terror and deterrence, was used in some instances. In the case of "Siôn Y Gof", the celebrated Dylife murderer of 1721, tradition asserts that he was obliged to build the very frame inside which his remains were found in 1938. Not all such executed criminals were suffered by those in their localities to endure such ignominy: John Thomas, an executed robber, was cut down in 1777, though his widow was acquitted of committing the offence.[55] Such an intervention might not have been possible in Pembroke, where in 1801 David Duckfield's body was apparently displayed on a gibbet some 30 feet high.[56] Anatomization of the corpse, i.e. its dissection by surgeons rather than burial, was introduced by the Murder Act of 1752. It makes some appearances in the Great Sessions records in cases of homicide of a very grave nature, such as the murder committed by Lewis Lewis in Breconshire in 1784. Lewis had hidden the body in a pool, but it emerged some seven months later, obliging Lewis to burn the remains and scatter them on his garden.[57]

Of forms of established but less severe punishment centred on the body there is evidence in the Quarter Sessions rolls of Welsh counties. In Denbighshire, for example, presentments were made of Wrexham Regis for not having stocks and a ducking stool in 1710, Ruthin for lack of stocks, pillory and ducking chair a year later and Bromfield hundred for not having a "very much wanted" ducking stool in 1730. Whether the neglect of provision revealed here indicates that such instruments were less used than they might have been, or whether they simply reveal a reluctance of local authorities to commit expenditure to them is not clear. There is also an account from the same county for whipping and burning in the hand in 1731. This latter phrase refers to the practice of branding offenders, both to warn the public against them and to prevent them claiming good character in any subsequent prosecutions. It originally was as brutal a sentence as it sounds, but later the "burning" could be a largely symbolic element. In Merionethshire around mid-century we have references to stocks at Vaerdre, Tywyn, Harlech and Dolgellau, a whipping post at Tywyn and a pillory at Bala.[58] Evidence from Breconshire provides more detail of the administration of whipping, one case from 1785 specifying that a minute should be left between each of the fifty lashes ordered by the court. The traditional formulation of such penalties as those mentioned here as simply "corporal" has been avoided here, for, as we saw in the last chapter, such public displays were intended to expose offenders to the local community, that they might suffer shame as well as pain and that their characters would be made known. The connection is made explicit in the 1754 case of Anne Thomas, excused whipping because of her pregnancy, it being ordered that:

> she shall stand the next three Markett days in the most publick market place within ye Town of Brecon for a whole hour each day with ye Word Thiefe wrote in large Characters on paper to be laid and pinned on her right shoulder to signify her said offences and as a mark of ignominy upon her.[59]

Newer forms of penality also make their appearance in eighteenth-century Wales. Transportation was a punishment which had precursors in earlier punishments of ostracism such as that of exile which was mentioned in Chapter 1, but which also incorporated elements of labour consonant with the needs of an expanding imperial presence. It had been placed on a firm and structured statutory footing in 1717 and had thereafter established itself as a dominant form of "secondary" punishment, i.e. one which spanned the considerable gap between execution and whipping. The implementation of the sentence saw Welsh convicts moved from their places of conviction, originally by local commercial agents and using, where possible, sea as opposed to land transport as the cheaper alternative, to ports like Bristol and Liverpool for shipment abroad. The destination was originally America until the War of Independence in 1776 ended that possibility. After 1787 Australia, of course, became the point of disembarkation. Unusually, Elizabeth Thomas was transported from Brecon in 1759 for 7 years "It being at her own request to Avoid Corporal Punishment". In the years between the closure of America and the First Fleet sailing to Botany Bay, and indeed for many years thereafter, prisoners sentenced to transportation might be obliged to spend the time of their sentence confined to the "hulks", decommissioned sailing vessels permanently moored at Woolwich and elsewhere. Welsh prisoners like the three from Brecon sent to the "Ceres" on the Thames were amongst those who suffered this fate.[60]

The development of incarceration as a penalty, to which the crisis in transportation and the experience of the hulks was to be a contributory factor, is a matter on which the records relating to Wales shed some interesting light. We noted in the last chapter that Houses of Correction, those curious hybrids between workhouses and prisons, were already in existence in some counties by the eighteenth century. In 1709 Samuel Booth, the Keeper of the Wrexham House of Correction proposed to teach 30 poor children aged 10 or above to spin "Jersey" and then to employ them after a year at the same rates as Chester spinners. Spinning seems to have been a much used occupation within such institutional settings, for we find it in the Forden House of Industry in 1797, with "confinement in the crib" as a punishment for not performing the task, and in Montgomery House of Correction in the nineteenth century.[61] The House of Correction, in addition to those considered idle and those who had committed minor offences, was at times used for the control of those with mental disorders at a time before asylum provision was common. William Mireck of Glamorganshire was held in such an institution in 1729 "for being visibly disordered in his senses and has lately behaved himself disorderly to several persons". During the building of a House of Correction in Denbighshire in 1773 one mentally disordered prisoner, Luke James, was confined in the County Gaol, and a remarkable letter written by him describing the experience of his treatment there survives. The County Gaol in Montgomery in 1803 held three lunatics, one of whom, a double murderer, was eventually removed to Bedlam, the specialist Bethlehem hospital for the mentally disordered in London.[62]

The County Gaols, provision of which had become part of the responsibility of Welsh local administrations after the extension of the English shiring system, also came in for attention in the eighteenth century. In some cases we may trace concern with the conditions and experience of incarceration to a period well before the publication of John Howard's *The State of the Prisons* in 1777, an event so often seen as the turning point for prison reform. Indeed, from the first half of the century Welsh figures associated with the Society for Promoting Christian Knowledge (SPCK), notably John Vaughan of Carmarthenshire and his friend Sir John Philips of Pembrokeshire, had urged penal reform. In 1725 the Society resolved that a "Copy of each of such Welch Books as the Society have in store be added to the Packets sent to the Prisons in North and South Wales".[63] Other initiatives in improving conditions also predated Howard's work. Proposals were made as early as 1765 for rebuilding the Merionethshire Gaol, an institution in relation to which a grant had been made to the gaoler for the upkeep of poor prisoners since 1707. Howard himself in the course of his visitations had found new building at Ruthin, Dolgellau, Cardigan and Cardiff. He found few prisoners within the buildings, however. Carmarthenshire's County Gaol, itself soon to be rebuilt by local architect John Nash, was by far the most populous of these Welsh institutions, with 26 prisoners (of whom 16 were debtors) in 1774.[64] It is interesting to note the reference to Wales within the seminal Penitentiary Act of 1779, in the drafting of which Howard had played a leading role. This Act, which proposed the construction of two national penitentiaries, was passed in reaction to the suspension of transportation and, though never implemented, it proved to be a ground-breaking measure in the history of central government penal provision. It prescribed a maximum of two inmates a year to come from all Welsh Great Sessions dispositions, as opposed to, for example, ten from the Norfolk Assize Circuit alone.[65]

It has been noted earlier that international affairs could change the nature of the response to domestic criminality. It could also bring in new categories of detainees; in 1779 there were 56 French and 37 American prisoners of war held at Pembroke. After 31 had escaped in 1797, supposedly with the assistance of love-smitten local girls, the remainder were removed to Portsmouth.[66]

The demographic, social and legal changes which the eighteenth century witnessed had their impact on the enforcement of the criminal law and its punishment. Yet, as we have seen, it is still too early to witness in Wales a complete retreat from an earlier pattern of dispute settlement which might operate outside the courtroom and which encompassed such matters as self-help and compensation. Whilst it is tempting to privilege either the changes, such as those discussed in the last paragraph, or the apparent underlying stability of the older methods within the account, it is clear that both are significant factors in our narrative. Simple Whiggist tales of progress or an antithetical antiquarian excavation for persistent tradition both ignore the fact that major drivers in the use of the criminal justice system include mentalities of law enforcers and victims, as well as practical efficiency and economics. Such matters will change, remain, combine and recombine to different extents, in different individuals, places and times. That remains the case as we turn to examine the nineteenth century.

Notes

1 S. and B. Webb, *English Prisons under Local Government* (London: Longmans, Green & Co., 1922) p. 204.
2 For Great Sessions, see www.llgc.org.uk/sesiwn_fawr/index_s.htm and N. Woodward, "Burglary in Wales, 1730–1830: evidence from the Great Sessions" *Welsh History Review*, 24 (2008a): 60; "Seasonality and sheep-stealing: Wales 1730–1830" *Agricultural History Review*, 56 (2008b): 25; "Horse stealing in Wales 1730–1830" *Agricultural History Review*, 57 (2009): 70. See also K. Watson, "Women, violent crime and criminal justice in Georgian Wales" *Continuity and Change* 28 (2013): 1. For the Carmarthen Gaol database, see www.welshlegalhistory.org/carms-felons-register.php.
3 Denbighshire Archives, *Enrolling the Past: A Description of Denbighshire Quarter Sessions Rolls, 1706–1800* (CD-Rom, Denbigh, 2003) Introduction.
4 See the analyses in Woodward, "Burglary", "Sheep stealing", "Horse stealing".
5 D. Howell, *The Rural Poor in Eighteenth-Century Wales* (Cardiff: University of Wales Press, 2000) p. 232.
6 Ibid., p. 214, *Unrolling the Past*, Introduction.
7 Howell, *Rural Poor*, p. 225.
8 Ibid., p. 190.
9 *Unrolling the Past*, Introduction.
10 Jenkins, *Foundations of Modern Wales*, pp. 333–4, Howell, *Rural Poor*, pp. 192–193, Watkin, *Legal History*, p. 164. The Crigyll wreckers were sufficiently notorious to

be accorded their customary title ("lladron Crigyll") when they stripped the Earl of Chester almost a century later; see *The Times*, 30 October 1867.

11 For the poem, see E.G. Millward (ed.), *Blodeugerdd Barddas o Gerddi Rhydd y Ddeunawfed Ganrif* (Llandybïe: Barddas, 1991) p. 70. For Morris's work see D. Bick and P.W. Davies, *Lewis Morris and the Cardiganshire Mines* (Aberystwyth: Immel Publishing, 1994). Incidentally, mining gave rise to other kinds of prosecution: see the early proceedings for polluting a watercourse in 1731, NLW GS 4/889.

12 Howell, *Rural Poor*, pp. 205–206, cf. the county/borough dispute in Cardigan in 1729, ibid., p. 207, S. Howard, "Riotous community: crowds, politics and society in Wales, *c.* 1700–1840" *The Welsh History Review* 20 (2001): 656 at p. 665.

13 T. Jones, *Rioting in North East Wales 1536–1918* (Wrexham: Bridge Books, 1997) p. 30.

14 Howard, "Riotous community", pp. 669–672.

15 Ibid., pp. 670, 664

16 Ibid., pp. 665–667.

17 Ibid., p. 667, W. Spurrell, *Carmarthen and its Neighbourhood* (Carmarthen: Dyfed County Council, 1879, repr. 1995) p. 144, D.J.V. Jones, *Before Rebecca: Popular Protests in Wales 1793–1835* (London: Allen Lane, 1973) Ch. 5.

18 See Jones, *Before Rebecca*, Ch. 1.

19 M. Löffler, *Welsh Responses to the French Revolution: Press and Public Discourse 1989–1802* (Cardiff: University of Wales Press, 2012) pp. 110, 173–174.

20 For the cases, ibid., pp. 105–106, 129.

21 See Howell, *Rural Poor*, p. 183.

22 Ibid., pp. 106–107.

23 G. Lamoine (ed.), *Charges to the Grand Jury 1689–1803*, Camden Fourth Series Volume 43 (London: Offices of the Royal Historical Society, 1992) p. 447.

24 B. Ellis, "The conveyance of vagrants across Montgomeryshire 1787–1806" *Montgomeryshire Collections* (2010) 98: 55.

25 *Unrolling the Past*, Introduction.

26 Ceredigion Archives QS/OB/4, p. 4.

27 G. Parry, *Launched to Eternity: Crime and Punishment 1700–1900* (Aberystwyth: National Library of Wales, 2001) pp. 11–12.

28 For the manorial court and poaching, see Howell, *Rural Poor*, p. 195; for a Court Leet, see, e.g., G.E. Evans, *Aberystwyth and its Court Leet* (Aberystwyth: Welsh Gazette, 1902).

29 Parry, *Launched to Eternity*, p. 15, Howell, *Rural Poor*, pp. 226–227.

30 Howell, *Rural Poor*, p. 233.

31 Humphreys, *Crisis of Community*, pp. 217–218.

32 Jones, *Before Rebecca*, p. 5.

33 K. Williams-Jones, *A Calendar of the Merioneth Quarter Sessions Rolls Vol I 1733–1765* (Merioneth: Merioneth County Council, 1965) pp. 109, 164.

34 Ceredigion Archives QS/OB/4, p. 6.

35 Watkin, *Legal History*, pp. 159–160.

36 The subject is admirably dealt with by Suggett in *History of Magic*, Ch. 4.

37 For Darcy, see Parry, *Launched to Eternity*, p. 16, for the cheese ordeal, Suggett, *History of Magic*, p. 78, for the mirror, Humphreys, *Crisis of Community*, p. 224, for the toad case (from 1871!), see R.W. Ireland, "First catch your toad: medieval attitudes to ordeal and battle" *Cambrian Law Review* (1980) 11: 50.

38 Suggett, *History of Magic*, p. 88; compare the use of the pillory against Daniel James in 1789 at http://history.powys.org.uk/history/common/pillory.html.

39 Suggett, *History of Magic*, Ch. 6 and pp. 130–131.

40 Parry, *Launched to Eternity*, p. 15, Woodward, "Horse stealing" p. 102.

41 Howell, *Rural Poor*, p. 233.

42 I am indebted to Rachael Jones for this information.

43　The original Act was 4 Geo. II c.26, the exposition 6 Geo. II c.14. For Raymond, see D. Mellinkoff, *The Language of the Law* (Boston, MA: Little Brown, 1963) p. 133.

44　Ceredigion Archives QS/OB/4, p. 8.

45　Jones, *Rioting in North East Wales*, p. 40.

46　Jones, "Welsh Language in Local Government" pp. 201–202.

47　Williams-Jones, *Calendar*, pp. 171, 229. And fees of 13s/4d at pp. 245, 254. For the Great Sessions, see Suggett, "Welsh language" p. 164 and note.

48　Quoted in Williams-Jones, *Calendar*, p. xxii.

49　H. Lloyd-Jones, "The Glanareth murder" *Transactions of the Honourable Society of Cymmrodorion* (1948) p. 271, Parry, *Launched to Eternity*, p. 23.

50　Watson, "Women, crime and justice" *passim*.

51　Williams-Jones, *Calendar*, p. xli, Humphreys, *Crisis of Community*, pp. 244–245.

52　Woodward, "Horse stealing" p. 84.

53　Supra p. 38.

54　See P. Rawlings, *Crime and Power* (Harlow: Longman, 1999) for discussion of the figures.

55　NLW GS 4/58/8.

56　R. Rose, *Pembroke People* (London: Otterquill Books, 2000) p. 75.

57　NLW GS 4/388/6.

58　See R.O. Denbighshire, *Unrolling the Past*, Introduction, Williams-Jones, *Calendar*, pp. 148, 220, 243, 257, 280.

59　Powys Digital History Project, *Crime and Punishment*.

60　Ibid. See generally D. Beddoe: *Welsh Convict Women* (Barry: S. Williams, 1979), "Carmarthenshire women and criminal transportation to Australia 1787–1852" *The Carmarthenshire Antiquary* 13 (1974): 65, Owen, *From Merioneth to Botany Bay*, pp. 10, 32–33, J.R. Williams, *Sentenced to Hell: The Story of Men and Women Transported from North Wales 1730–1878* (Pwllheli: Llygad GwalchCyf, 2011).

61　*Unrolling the Past*, A. Thomas Ellis (ed.), *Wales: An Anthology* (London: Fontana Press, 1980) p. 220, A. and J. Welton, *The Story of Montgomery* (Almeley: Logaston Press, 2003) p. 126. A weaver was appointed as Master of the Brecon House of Correction in 1781, and see D. Davies, *Law and Disorder in Breconshire 1750–1880* (Brecon: Evans) p. 14.

62　Lewis, "Documents illustrating the County Gaol" p. 240, K. Matthias, "The mad Irishman's letter" *Clwyd Historian*, Welton, *Montgomery*, 64 (2011): 123–124.

63　M. Clement, *Correspondence and Minutes of the SPCK Relating to Wales 1699–1740* (Cardiff: University of Wales Press, 1952) p. 294, Watkin, *Legal History*, p. 160.

64　Williams-Jones, *Calendar*, p. lxix, J. Howard, *The State of the Prisons* (1777, repr. Abingdon: Routledge, 1977).

65　19 Geo. III c.74 s.xxv.

66　Rose, *Pembroke People*, pp. 345–346. C. Lloyd, *A History of Napoleonic and American Prisoners of War 1756–1816* (Woodbridge: Antique Collectors Club, 2007) Ch. 4 gives an original total of 400 prisoners in the "Golden Tower Prison, near Pembroke" after the French invasion (p. 65).

4 The nineteenth century

The uniform – and the white gloves

The demographic and social changes which we noted in the last chapter continued apace in the nineteenth century. Statistical analysis shows a significant growth in population, an increase in the size and significance of towns, a revolution in transport and mobility, the rise of the chapel at the expense of the church, the replacement of agriculture by industry as the dominant source of employment and an erosion in the dominance of the Welsh language.[1] In legal terms, the Great Sessions were abolished in 1830 and their work incorporated into a revised Assize system. The modern rules of evidence and the role of witnesses and counsel were being standardized, and the "new police" were introduced throughout the jurisdiction. In relation to punishment there was what has been described as a "revolution", with the dismantling of the "Bloody Code" and other forms of public punishment of the body, the discontinuation of transportation and the apparently inexorable rise in both the use of, and central government control over, imprisonment.[2] In the nineteenth century, then, even if it had not happened in the eighteenth, we might anticipate that in the administration of criminal justice in Wales everything would have changed.

But did it? In 1851 the urbane Mr Justice Talfourd interrupted an Assize sitting in Carmarthen to ask whether the jury understood English, only to be surprised and alarmed by their reply;[3] in 1871 P.C. David Davies found great difficulty in preventing a crowd in Newcastle-Emlyn from giving beer to John Foster who was held in stocks, first by his feet and then by his wrists, for six hours;[4] a year later, one Corry Lee was convicted at Llandeilo in that she did:

> by using subtle craft and device deceive and impose and impose [sic] upon one John Williams towit [sic] by pretending that she could cure the said John Williams' Son of fits to which he was subject by tying a garter into three Knots and using a small quantity of earth taken from over the grave of a young maiden and other similar acts and whereby she induced the said John Williams to pay her the said Corry Lee the sum of one shilling;[5]

and at some unspecified time and place in the second half of the nineteenth century (our narrator is reliable, his imprecision here quite deliberate) a murder was settled by compensation rather than by prosecution.[6] And Wales was apparently crime free, "Cymru Lân" ("pure Wales"), "Gwlad y menyg gwynion" ("land of white gloves"), though Taffy, the Welshman, was notoriously "a thief".[7] This chapter will have to confront the paradoxes suggested here. As with earlier chapters, we will have cause to question a simple linear narrative of overthrown paradigms and inevitable progress. We must explore these matters more closely.

Whilst a detailed consideration of demographic changes clearly lies outside the scope of this book, nonetheless some features of the process of interest to our main theme may be briefly noted.[8] First then it is clear that in the formation of urban and industrial centres the influence of the more traditional rural background of the workers who had been drawn to them did not disappear instantly. The report on Merthyr (whose "China" district became a byword for criminality), which was compiled for the Commission on the State of Education in Wales in 1847, is interesting in this respect. The whole sounds slightly disappointed that the town had not revealed its signal horrors, its compiler relating that "I did not encounter a single disturbance, nor a single drunken man". But it reveals the complex and particular character of the developing town and the challenge to law and order created by the traditional stabilities within its population rather than its novelty:

> The workmen, who are continually immigrating, live together very much in clans, e.g. the Pembrokeshire men in one quarter, the Carmarthenshire men in another and so on. This kind of clanship makes them oppose every obstacle to the detection of offenders, who flock to Merthyr from all parts of Wales.[9]

Such established associations also presumably explain the appearance in the town of popular punishment of a kind which, as we will see, is more usually connected with the countryside, such as the *ceffyl pren* used against the Merthyr adulteress Anne Harman in 1834.[10] Indeed despatch to the industrial areas or other distant occupations, as the report mentioned above seems to evidence, might indeed be in itself a form of communal punishment, the fate of those who had been driven from their home villages by the hostility of their neighbours. As Parry-Jones, reflecting on his experience of rural life in the nineteenth century, put it:

> Any member who transgressed [rural society's] standards and brought shame not only on his own family but on the larger "family" as well, had to make the one inevitable recompense and that was to leave it to join the army, the navy, migrate to the coal-mines, or else stay on to receive the full impact of the mounting wrath of the offended society. Oh yes, it applied sanctions![11]

Whilst this discussion makes clear that a simple urban/rural division within Welsh society is unsustainable in the earlier nineteenth century, nonetheless such a trope can be found in at least some of the discourse which emerges around criminality in Wales as the century progresses. This suggested that Wales, or at least such parts of Wales as remained pristine, untouched by the vices brought by urbanization and immigration, was immune from criminality. The promotion of this idea, not least by the minister and M.P. Henry Richard, was, of course, far removed from earlier English representations of a factional or lawless region. In this formulation, Wales became "the land of white gloves", a nation whose absence from (serious) crime was marked by the presentation of the gloves (the symbolic opposite of the black cap), to the Assize judge faced with no criminal business. The formula is one which has been mentioned in the Introduction, but some discussion is needed here.[12] It must be stated at the outset, however, that it is impossible accurately to measure the extent to which a perceived absence of serious crime in Wales was simply down to underreporting rather than an essential respect for the law. At least one Victorian commentator, sensitive to allegations that concealment was the cause, conducted empirical research to argue that this was an error.[13] Yet, to what extent, for example, the spread and rigour of Nonconformist religiosity acted as a curb on anti-social conduct is a matter impossible of proof, but its effects should certainly not be discounted. It is also clear, however, that even such crime as did occur might be dealt with, as the quotation from Parry-Jones suggests, in a manner which left it outside the jurisdiction of the superior, or indeed any, court. Aside from enforced migration we will see at a number of points below that other means of addressing wrongs – compensation (even in cases of homicide), intervention of religious figures, popular penality such as the *ceffyl pren* – and the well-known "independence" of Welsh juries, certainly diverted cases from court which might otherwise have got there.

If "real Welshmen" were to be portrayed as free from the taint of crime, then such crime as might be undeniable would, in this formulation, be attributable to "outsiders" – vagrants (in particular after the famine, "the Irish"), navvies, travelling gangs (their job made easier by the work of those navvies) and those warped by the lack of traditional constraint, the speed and anonymity of that "untraditional" social environment, the urban sprawl. Paradoxically this self-generated view of the law-abiding "true Welshman" was not always echoed by those to the east to whom it was at least partially directed. In an interesting aggregation the Welsh were normally unproblematically discussed alongside the English when they behaved themselves, but when they caused trouble they tended to be grouped together with the Irish![14]

Before pursuing such themes it may be as well to mention two events which produced representations of the state of Wales which had a significant effect on the administration of justice within the country. First, and most obviously, is the investigation into the operation of the Great Sessions in the Select Committee to enquire into the Administration of Justice in Wales, 1817–21 and the Commission of Enquiry into the Superior Courts of Common Law, 1829, the outcome of which investigations was the abolition of the distinct

Welsh Court in 1830. The underlying justification of assimilation was explained in the 1821 Report:

> However well adapted the Courts may have been in their origin to the circumstances of a country newly subdued, in which the English language was at the time almost unknown, having little or no means of communication with the seats of justice in England, and liable to all the jealousies of recent enmity, that the lapse of years, and the great changes that have taken place in the condition of Wales, have removed most, if not all, the reasons on account of which the institution of local jurisdiction were resorted to.

It would be fanciful to suggest that the dearth of criminal business before English Assize judges was a reaction to this abolition, but we should note the observation of the most informed of the historians of the court that there is "certainly some evidence to support the view that the Welsh regarded the Great Sessions as a national institution, worthy of preservation".[15]

As to the reaction to the second "external" assessment, the Report of the Education Commissioners of 1847, then there is considerable evidence of reaction to what was called the "*brad y llyfrau gleision*", the "treachery of the Blue Books". The report had conceded that the Welsh were largely immune from major crime, but had made adverse comments on the general status of their morality as a whole which seemed to traduce the whole country. The report was a significant event in nineteenth-century Welsh history generally, and I suggest that a sensitivity to accusations of stereotypical vice may have had at least some impact upon the subsequent rate of prosecutions and convictions, in particular in relation to what might loosely be termed "morals" offences (i.e. sexual wrongs, or those committed within a domestic context) in the second half of the century.[16]

We have already seen that vagrancy had long been regarded as a problem in Wales, and a generally more mobile population in the nineteenth century sharpened the focus on the issue. Moreover the Irish Famine of the "Hungry Forties", with the emigration to Welsh ports which resulted from it, came at a convenient time for Welsh polemicists to promote native virtue by demonising outsiders.[17] Vagrancy, since it was in effect simply poverty in the wrong place, was a genuine social problem, but also a conveniently loose one. Both a criminal offence in itself and a way of life associated generally with a more thoroughgoing criminal existence, vagrancy was presented as a social threat not only in the rural heartlands of Anglesey, Carmarthenshire and Cardiganshire, but also in the urban complexity of Merthyr's "China". Counties vied with each other to establish methods of dealing with vagrants that moved them onto their neighbours' territory, and the unpopularity and reputation of the displaced poor made them a target for the close attention of the police, once the new forces had been established.[18] Paradoxically, perhaps, there is at least some evidence to suggest that one of the other nineteenth-century "folk-devils", the railway navvy, was less intensively policed. These people too were itinerant, often young, outsiders associated with lawlessness, but were more discrete and controlled in their movement and residence. Although there were official interventions, in some cases following violent altercations between groups of workers with an ethnic dimension, such as at Penmaenmawr in 1846 or at Ferryside in 1851, it seems that criminality, if confined within the group might often be left to sort itself out.[19]

One other class of offence which could be blamed upon the corrupting effect of social change was prostitution, which was associated in particular (although not exclusively) with urban life.[20] Some areas, "China" again, or Friars' Fields in Newport for example, were notorious for prostitution which might be entrenched within particular families, whilst evidence from Wrexham and Welshpool shows groups of women following the army for trade.[21] Even smaller towns might support surprisingly large numbers of prostitutes, whose primary occupation was associated with other offences such as keeping brothels (of which there were apparently 20 in Merthyr alone in 1860) and the theft from the person committed by the women themselves or their "bullies".[22] The trade was well enough acknowledged in Carmarthen for a visiting surgeon from Stourbridge to ask for, and be given, directions from a policeman as to "where he could meet with some women of loose characters", whilst the assiduous record-keeping of Police Constable Williams in the same town in 1859–1860 gives us an insight into a world populated by women whose trade names ranged from the mundane ("Nell the Cockle Girl") to the exotic ("Santalena").[23] Forty years earlier the remarkably frank diary of Customs Officer Matthew Campbell describes the sex trade in Pembroke, where rewards could be potentially surprisingly high, though some of the girls involved were distressingly young.[24]

It is banal to observe that changing patterns of demography and industry, as well as tension between different national groups, had a part to play in some of the major instances of unrest, protest and riot which marked nineteenth-century Wales and which made the names of places like Merthyr and Newport known to people who had never seen the country. It is clear that in a work of this nature it will not be possible to do more than hint at the aetiology, morphology and significance of these various events to which we now turn. That each merits individual study is apparent, but it is comforting to report that we enter a subject which has been for the most part well explored by social historians of Wales, with the result that those who seek deeper analyses will be able to find them through the references supplied.

Some disturbances were rural ones, protests about such matters as enclosure, or the interference with customary rights. Amongst these latter were denials of title to the *tai unnos*, houses built on common land which, if completed overnight, were supposed to generate ownership, a right erroneously but significantly claimed to be derived from *Cyfraith Hywel*. One notable rural uprising, amongst other riots in the west in the early part of the century, was the series of disputes between 1820 and 1827 on Mynydd Bach (Cardiganshire) against the "improvements" of Augustus Brackenbury. The soubriquet which attached to the struggle, "*rhyfel y sais bach*"/"the war of the little Englishman", hints at the element of cultural conflict involved, whilst the presentation by the rioters of a copy of the fictitious "Turf Act", an attempt to arrogate legal form to customary claim, again shows the desire to legitimate the protest.[25]

Elements of theatre were also evident in the "Scotch Cattle" disturbances in the industrial areas of South Wales in the 1820s and '30s. Again, it may be misleading to dwell upon one manifestation of industrial unrest when it may be seen to form part of the broader history of popular protest recognized as such by contemporaries as well as by historians.[26] One such outbreak of tension was the South Wales strike of 1816 which had seen prosecutions for leaving employment as well as removal of individuals under Poor Law provisions as legal ploys to control activists. Yet the "Scotch Cattle", led by the "Bull" and dressed in skins and lowing like cows as they made their intimidatory nocturnal visits in order to enforce strikes and control access to jobs in the coal and iron industry, display that genius for ritualized "otherness" and performed solidarity which are so striking in nineteenth-century Welsh protest. Though rooted in the essentially pragmatic need for disguise, such activities have been seen by social historians as attempts to carry familiar rural mechanisms of communal control, such as the *ceffyl pren* to be discussed later, into the industrial landscape. It should not be thought, however, that the display was simply a form of benign street theatre, for the "Cattle" could be violent. Internal solidarity combined with fear of reprisals meant that it was hard for the authorities to gain information to lead to prosecution. In 1835, following the shooting of a woman in the attack on a house, three of the rioters were condemned to death despite the recommendation to mercy by the jury. One of them, Edward Morgan, was hanged before "three to four thousand spectators" at Monmouth. At the trial one of the witnesses had refused to give evidence in English.[27]

Morgan had urged that, whilst he was involved in the disturbances, he had not taken part in the shooting, and the popular unease over the execution reminds us of another execution, that of Richard Lewis, "Dic Penderyn", following the Merthyr Rising of 1831. The rioting was a product of many causes, not least a lowering of wages at the Cyfartha Ironworks, but including also wider issues of more general concern: the role of the Court of Requests in debt litigation, issues of free trade and of an emerging political radicalism. Famously, and apparently for the first time in Britain, the rioters raised a red flag in the proceedings. The ensuing violence outside the Castle Hotel claimed at least 16 lives lost to soldiers (disturbingly the exact figure remains unknown, though it was greater than those killed at Peterloo, a much more celebrated massacre). In the trials which followed, Richard Lewis and Lewis Lewis, the latter subsequently reprieved, were sentenced to death and others were transported or imprisoned. Despite a petition of over 11,000 names Dic Penderyn was hanged for wounding, declaring "O Arglwydd, dyma gamwedd" ("oh Lord, this is an injustice"), and doubts about the extent of his guilt ensured that he was seen, in the words of the historian John Davies, as "Wales's first working-class martyr".[28]

Radicalism in the 1830s was also witnessed in Chartist agitation in Wales, where a Working Men's Association had been formed in Carmarthen even before the "People's Charter" was published in 1839. In that year a riot broke out in the small town of Llanidloes in Montgomeryshire following the despatch of three Metropolitan policemen to arrest local activists implicated in meetings and damage to the new Caersws workhouse. Opposition to the new Poor Law of 1834 was a feature, too, of the Rebecca Riots to be discussed below. Other specifically local factors fed the Llanidloes rioting, and the disorder led ultimately to three participants being transported and others sentenced to imprisonment. Punitive bail conditions which could not be met by those subject to them were used as a way of engineering pre-trial detention for those regarded as dangerous. It has been argued that the Llanidloes disturbances were seized upon to discredit Chartism more generally.[29] It must have come as some surprise to the Inspector of Prisons to find prisoners in the County Gaol at Montgomery in 1839 sleeping two to a bed after the Llanidloes incident and further agitation at Newtown, where a rally of more than 2,000 assembled in that year. The Chartists, he reported, complained about the food, although they received a more liberal diet than other inmates.[30]

1839 was also the year of the Newport Rising, which involved action by thousands of armed miners and has been described as "the most serious insurrectionary movement in nineteenth-century Britain"[31] Some 20 to 30 rioters (again it is both remarkable and a disturbing testament to the nature of Government involvement that the exact number of casualties can still not be determined with confidence) were killed when soldiers fired into a crowd of demonstrators. The outcome of the disturbances was as dramatic as the events: the authorities swept up Chartists, as well as others such as strangers and beer-sellers. The authorities recruited informers and imprisoned suspects in the Newport union workhouse, whilst on the other side non-co-operation with the legal process and intimidation of witnesses threatened the success of prosecutions. Ultimately the trials were heard by a Special Commission, headed by Tindal LCJ, and three of the radicals, John Frost, Zephaniah Williams and William Jones, were sentenced to death for high treason and others transported. Although it seemed improbable initially, the Government, swayed apparently more by the legal concerns of Tindal about the conduct of the trial itself rather than by popular support for the men (more people signed a petition for their pardon than had signed the Chartists' National Petition) commuted the death sentences and the men sailed to Van Diemen's Land on the convict-ship *Mandarin*.[32] Newport had shown that Wales, or at least parts of Wales, was not quite as peaceful as it might seem, and the nature of the response and of the charges brought demonstrated the Government's concern to suppress popular unrest.

The concern was not only over the events in Newport, for also in 1839 trouble had broken out with an attack upon a tollhouse in Efailwen (Carms) in May. This was the beginning of a series of disturbances which lasted for some considerable time, though the main unrest had been quelled by late 1843, when three of the rioters were transported. The nocturnal torchlit assemblies of "Rebecca and her daughters", their name generally believed to be taken from the book of Genesis, their gender from the female attire worn by the male participants, had a number of targets.[33] Undoubtedly the proliferation of toll fees on turnpike roads was a source of grievance to struggling small farmers in the counties of the south-west who were obliged to use the roads to transport materials. But broader economic pressures, a resentment of the new Poor Law, complaints about the quality of rural Welsh justice and elements of political radicalism all fed into a mood of discontent. As to the seriousness of the uprising, the Westminster government was under no illusion. The Home Secretary, Sir James Graham, expressed his fear that Wales might become "a second Ireland", and the response to the events was proportionate to its perceived gravity. It involved not only a cavalry charge through the streets of Carmarthen but also the drafting in of Metropolitan Police officers.[34] The presence of the latter was significant both for the subsequent development of policing within Wales and also, to a lesser extent, by the contribution of their personnel to the reformation of Welsh prison life.[35] *The Report of the Commissioners of Inquiry for South Wales* of 1844, together with certain portions of the report on Municipal Corporations of almost a decade earlier, as well as the celebrated Education Commissioners' opinions of 1847 are valuable correctives to a view which suggests that the administration of public life and legal affairs within Wales had become tangential to the London government after the abolition of Great Sessions in 1830.[36] Rebecca was a significant episode in Welsh criminal history, not least because it was *rural* disorder and that it used, as we shall see, techniques and symbolism appropriate to Welsh rural practice. A number of tensions – town/country, agriculture/industry, local/central, "traditional"/"modern" as well as Welsh/ English – can, without, I think, too much artifice, be read into these theatrical but very real and sometimes very violent events of the Rebecca riots.

It is probable that it was the tradition of Rebecca, rather than the earlier *ceffyl pren* gatherings upon which the riots themselves drew, that led to the use of female clothing being donned in subsequent mass disturbances. It was apparent in the 1856 Talargoch (Flintshire) lead mine strike and again (with explicit invocation of the Carmarthenshire events) in the round of protests which surfaced sporadically from the 1850s into the twentieth century, against enforcement of fishery laws on the Upper Wye.[37]

The parallel with Ireland, noted above in respect of Rebecca, is also worth following in later disturbances, including the "Tithe Wars" which we are about to consider. Whilst the Irish in Wales might be resented as vagrants or feared as rivals for the jobs of native workers (a sentiment, for example, which led to anti-Irish riots in Tredegar in 1882),[38] it has been suggested that the "Tithe Wars" tapped into fears of disorder of a kind familiar from over the Irish sea. Tithe protest itself had an earlier Irish precursor and, during the period of the unease, the Irish radical Michael Davitt spoke in North Wales. At a time when "Home Rule" ideas were circulating, this was uncomfortable for the establishment.[39]

The "Tithe Wars" deserve our attention as representing another rural phenomenon which attracted considerable social support and a deeply felt grievance by "respectable" Welsh rural society. Tithes, payable in money rather than kind since legislation of 1836, were mulcts originally to support the Anglican church, though the profits of many had by the nineteenth century fallen into lay hands. The fees were paid by tenant farmers, a great many of whom were themselves Nonconformists. Refusal to pay resulted in forced sales of the defaulters' belongings, and disturbances connected with such events broke out in North Wales in 1886–1888. In one of these the Riot Act was translated into Welsh by an Abergele Police Sergeant and read to the crowd.[40] Despite a change in the law in 1891 designed to ameliorate the position, there were further disturbances in Cardiganshire in 1893. Again, we see the element of theatrical display in such agitation, as at an occasion at Cwm Eithin (Denbs) where a later account has the auctioneers obliged to wear their coats inside-out "to show their repentance".[41] Again, too, we see the concern of central government, which cannot have been assuaged by the rowdy displays in court proceedings which followed the Cardiganshire disturbances.[42]

Figure 4.1 A photograph of the Constabulary and Lancers at Llanfair Talhaearn during the Tithe War, 1888.
Courtesy Denbighshire Archive Service.

In a case of wounding in the midst of the 1893 disturbances, the defendant's acquittal was greeted by "round upon round of cheering", followed by an assurance from the defendant's representative that the victim would receive "ample recompense".[43] This detail, only incidentally recorded, opens a window onto many of the subterranean complexities of the nineteenth-century Welsh legal system. To the role of the jury we must return later, but for now it is necessary to recall the tradition of extra-curial dispute resolution which we have charted consistently in previous chapters. The termination of a criminal case in favour of compensation is by no means unique and indeed we find it explicitly enjoined by Justices of the Peace in a number of cases.[44] I do not know how often it is to be found in England at this time, though I do know that it has not been sufficiently examined there. In Wales, I have no doubt, it reveals more than a certain flexibility on the boundary between "civil" and "criminal" jurisdiction and taps into the tradition of compensation well established in custom. At the outset of this chapter we noted its use in a homicide case ("a family of considerable means was alleged to have become poor, a few cottagers were alleged to have found it not altogether an ill wind"[45]). Compensation still afforded a means of dealing with wrongdoing in a way unimagined by the movers of the "penal revolution" which dominated nineteenth-century punishment practice.

But so did other things. Arbitration on an issue of interpersonal violence could be conducted within the chapel, keeping "clear of the court of law ... to make it a matter of church discipline".[46] Most dramatic of all, particularly in West Wales, was the *ceffyl pren*, the "wooden horse" which we have noted as a model for Rebecca's performances. This nocturnal display of mass disapproval, often including the "carrying" of the "offender" either in person or in effigy, belongs to a wider tradition of "ridings" or "rough music" but, in its precise morphology, its presumed (by some contemporaries at least) connection with the laws of Hywel Dda, and in its longevity as a social custom it deserves comment as a specifically Welsh institution.[47] It was, of course, thoroughly disapproved of by those who subscribed to a notion of "respectability" within the nineteenth century which sought to suppress all manner of rowdy public performances, but carried a particular threat to an increasingly rule-defined criminal justice system. Serious enough when used as an alternative to the criminal process, it became more so when used as an adverse comment upon that system (as when invoked against Elizabeth Gibbs, acquitted by a Carmarthen jury on charges of poisoning in 1851[48]) or in direct opposition to it (as when it was used against informers). We have records of attempts by the police and a local landowner to prevent the staging of a *ceffyl pren* in 1861[49] and prosecutions of those who did participate in them, notably in Cardiganshire in 1837.[50] Instances of such "outrages" continue throughout the century, and the tradition can even be seen, according to one of the subject's most astute commentators, reworked in actions taken against strike-breakers in industrial disputes in Wales in the twentieth century.[51]

Yet, while it is proper to note the longevity of traditions of "informal" dispute settlement, we cannot ignore the very real changes occurring within the criminal justice system, in particular the establishing of the police and the extending ambit of the criminal law. These two developments are likely to be have been significant not simply in that the police might seek to suppress alternative methods of dispute settlement, or that the law might provide more summary and immediate means of redressing grievances, but also because they increasingly normalized the apparent centrality of the role of the state in the maintenance of order. As David Jones put it, "all over Wales attachments to older concepts of order, memories of ancient codes of behaviour, and established forms of community policing were passing away .... Gradually, official methods of dealing with crimes and of resolving conflicts gained wider popularity. This "penetration of the state into the parish" occurred at different speeds amongst different social groups and in different communities".[52] And just as it would be wrong to emphasize the *continuity* of process over the changes which took place, so too would it be to leave the reader with the impression, which may have been suggested by the preceding pages, that the paradigm of nineteenth-century Welsh criminality was the communal uprising. It was not, and we must turn our attention to the more mundane experiences of crime and punishment in the comments which follow.

"Drunks, both male and female, were the archetypal criminals of late-nineteenth-century Wales" says David Jones, charting the rise in prosecutions returned to the Home Office in the second half of the century.[53] He stresses that these statistics reflect enforcement policies rather than necessarily a simple increase in events of drunkenness, but there is no doubt that such offences (and we are generally dealing with street drunkenness, visible to the new police forces, rather than the private excesses of the more privileged) are significant in bringing considerable numbers of people into contact with the criminal justice system. They also, through the programme of construction and renovation of lock-ups which accompanied the formation of police forces, served to normalize the experience of incarceration, which, as we will see continued to develop significantly as the century proceeded.[54] On the other side of the coin from the offences of drunkenness were prosecutions for breaches of the licensing regulations. An otherwise unremarkable case from Cardigan in 1870 highlights an interesting issue, as the meaning of a Welsh phrase used by the defendant was debated before the court to establish whether it implied that customers were served in unlicensed premises.[55] The totemic Welsh Sunday Closing Act of 1881, an amendment of the criminal law specifically limited to Wales, seems to have had rather more of an impact on Welsh constitutional history than it did on the drinking habits of the nation.[56]

Official statistics on offences of violence in nineteenth-century Wales have been analysed by David Jones, although again it must be borne in mind that these statistics record a very complex and changing amalgam of events attitudes and mechanisms, which means that they must be used with extreme caution. Nonetheless Jones's picture is of violence increasing from around the

1820s but experiencing a significant decline towards the end of the century, and a greater concentration of violence in urban rather than in rural areas.[57] Certainly the reputation of Wales as a whole seems to have been as a relatively peaceful place, though certain events or localities might dent that reputation. I would make a couple of observations which seem worthy of note and which may (I leave this as a hypothesis for the historians of English criminal justice to test) have a specifically Welsh dimension. First, I am struck by the "communal" nature of responses to serious crime, the large and vocal crowds which could assemble inside and outside courts, outside police stations and prisons in which suspects were held, at railway stations to catch sight of the hangman even when, after 1868, hanging, very rarely carried out by then in any event, was conducted in secrecy. I am fully aware that in England too there was considerable, on occasions massive, public attendance at hangings in particular, and it may be that the Welsh evidence is not unusual in this respect. But the feeling remains that in Wales condemnation (like shaming, like protest) was a communal event. So in Carmarthen in 1847 the Governor of the gaol waited for the child-killer Mary Hughes to be smuggled into the gaol at 2.30 in the morning to avoid the townspeople.[58] "Great crowds" gathered in the same town in 1889 to see the hangman Berry disembark from his train on his way to hang David Rees (which he did, bizarrely, "unostentatiously dressed in a plain suit of dark clothes and wearing a red Turkish fez"[59]), and vast numbers attended not only the execution of Matthew Francis of Newport but all the preliminary processes, including the railway stations he passed through on his way to trial at Monmouth.[60] It is true also that such mass gatherings were not restricted to cases of violence, which is primarily where they have been noted in England. We have seen them in trials of cases of popular disorder earlier and they seem to have particularly enjoyed the scandal of bigamy cases. In the case of the "electro-biologist" Mrs Poole, prosecuted in 1868 after commanding 14 mesmerized men to attack a sceptical audience member armed with a hat pin, the public interest seems to have obliged the court to move to a larger venue purely to satisfy their amused curiosity. Such public engagement serves to situate crimes and their consequences within a specific and important social setting even within a recognisably "modern" state context.[61]

Second, I wish to make a comment about violence within the family, including infanticide, and sexual offences. These are crimes in which we might expect a considerable number of offences to remain undiscovered and unreported and indeed this appears to have been the case. But the point I wish to make here is that there is some element of social judgement at play in such cases. We will investigate shortly the concept of jury equity more generally, but it would appear that it was particularly marked in these offences. Evidence from Carmarthenshire suggests that it was very difficult in that county at least to secure a conviction even for the misdemeanour of concealment of birth (rather than the felony of murder), even when the former at least seems clearly to have been committed, when young children were found dead. The evidence of convictions in such cases for Wales as a whole, as for England, admittedly seems rather more ambiguous. Sexual offences seem routinely to have been downgraded by Grand Juries (who were approached beforehand) and/or petty juries, while domestic violence cases might be "compromised" by magistrates, sometimes with the assistance of others present in court. It is easy to reach for standard explanations of "sympathy" for the accused, particularly in the childbirth cases, but such ideas are hard to maintain: the farmers who sat on the juries were the very people who would fire their servant girls if they became pregnant, thereby inducing the commission of the offence. The issues are more subtle and interesting than this. It seems that, even in the second half of the nineteenth century, Wales, or at least some sections of it, knew of a class of wrongdoing more properly to be made subject to communal, rather than arbitral judgment or control, and of a category of behaviour which was felt to be more the preserve of the world of shame (communal as well as individual) than of the world of guilt.[62]

Again it should be pointed out that there is a danger of regarding such attitudes, important as they are, as universal, ancient and unchallenged. It seems to me that a desire to keep "morals" offences out of the Assize courts with their alien judiciary may actually have been strengthened in the nineteenth century as a reaction to the slur of the Blue Books. It also remains true that a number of such cases involving intra-familial violence did come to trial and conviction, not least one remarkable case of manslaughter of a child by her parents. The trial of Evan and Hannah Jacob took place in Carmarthen in 1870 after the death of their daughter Sarah, "The Welsh Fasting Girl". Sarah had starved whilst under the supervision of local doctors and London nurses who were testing the claim that she was nourished by faith alone. The proceedings drew immense national interest and looked set, in a prosecution initiated, significantly, by the London government rather than local authorities, to become a test case for the competing claims of science and religion, rationalism and (rural Welsh) superstition. That such broader considerations ultimately became lost in the proceedings speaks much of the stubbornness of the local magistracy and the pragmatism of both the counsel and the jury at the trial.[63] It should perhaps also be mentioned here that nineteenth-century Wales did witness other celebrated and significant legal controversies concerning matters of belief, notably over the question of the propriety of post-mortem cremation.[64]

When property crime is examined, we find again that theft retained its traditional targets of household goods, money and (in rural areas) livestock. Again it is also well represented in our statistics. Jones's study of the recorded patterns of property crimes is detailed and suggests significant differences in the quantity of urban and rural offending within Wales, the latter being lower, and, interestingly, between England and Wales, the latter being again the lower.[65] At the risk of labouring the point I would again remind the reader that such official figures are the result of a complex and malleable pattern of reporting and processing. They may record objective differences in crime rates or (and/or?) differences in social attitudes, in the practices of enforcement agencies or of opportunities for alternative resolution. Differences of demography and technology must certainly be acknowledged as variables in considering the nature as well as the extent of property crime, which, though it looks elemental and static, can be responsive to wider social change. So, for example, the coming of the railways from around mid-century had significant effects on the distribution of thieves. Drovers and merchants, who often carried considerable sums of money on remote roads when returning from the sales of their animals, became less vulnerable to robbery when their trade transferred to rail, although conversely theft of goods from railway wagons, particularly of coal, became notable in its turn. Similarly the bureaucracy of the new transport system allowed opportunities for embezzlement by railway employees, whilst the concentration of crowds at busy stations provided more regular hunting grounds for pickpockets, who, like the "thimble riggers" had previously traditionally operated primarily at fairs and sales.[66] Changes in the way goods were exposed for sale in shops in towns and cities allowed the development of techniques of shoplifting, which the Glamorgan magistrates in 1860 seemed to regard as an understandable response to temptation. It also seems to have been regarded as an offence which was to a large extent associated with juvenile offenders.[67] In the countryside, meanwhile, changes in the laws relating to the taking of ground game and fish led to many prosecutions for a variety of poaching offences. In such prosecutions the interests of Justices as landholders and as magistrates were often difficult to distinguish. The game laws were recognized as a source of continuing concern for tenant farmers as late as 1896, when the *Royal Commission on Land Holdings in Wales and Monmouthshire* reported.[68]

Two significant changes went hand in hand in the legal development of the nineteenth century in England and Wales generally. One of these is the significant expansion of the criminal law beyond its traditional concern with immediate wrong to person and property to cover such diverse activities as education, animal health and welfare, vaccination, employment obligations (over contracts, safety, service and pay), road traffic regulations and many, many other such matters. They are often termed "regulatory offences", indicative perhaps of a covert assumption of a distinction from "real" crime, committed by "real" criminals, yet they account for significant numbers of prosecutions. Sometimes these involved otherwise "respectable" defendants who might be surprised to see themselves appearing at the same tribunals as the "habitual" or "professional" criminals whose appearance as a topic for debate and concern was so marked in the second half of the century. A book of this kind cannot hope to investigate all such regulatory offences in detail, though the reader may be assured that David Jones, not the least of whose achievements was to ignore the distorting concentration on serious crime which has bedevilled the work of many others who have worked in this area, provides a useful account of the offences.[69] Suffice it to say that anyone who picks up, say, a bundle of summary convictions in a Welsh archive will meet many records of offences such as "furious driving", failing to have a name marked on a cart, or leaving a ship or other employment unlawfully. My own experience of Carmarthenshire records suggests that standard-form records of conviction often record the offence as committed, with splendid (and I suspect not accidental) imprecision, "contrary to the form of the statute". The increasing volume and complexity of criminal legislation seems too much for the magistrates and their clerks to navigate. I would add, too, that important pieces of early "environmental" statute law relating to pollution of watercourses as a result of discharge from mine workings drew in part on the experience of destruction of salmon fisheries, owned of course by the gentry, in Wales. It is also interesting to note that late-nineteenth-century statutes concerning regulations of workplaces such as mines, quarries and factories sometimes make express provision favouring the appointment of Welsh speakers as inspectors where their qualifications are equal to other candidates.[70]

Reference to the fact that the "regulatory" offences are for the most part subject to summary process alerts us to the second element of transition, alluded to briefly earlier. This was the move away from jury trial at Assize and Quarter Sessions. The distrust of Welsh jurors may also have accelerated the introduction of the stipendiary magistrate system into Wales, a move which began as early as 1843.[71]My feeling, unscientific and unsupported by statistical analysis as it is, is that such summary convictions tend rather to take the place of binding-over orders, which we have seen to have been so central an element in peacekeeping in Wales. Such orders still exist and are still used in the nineteenth century, but there is perhaps a sense that a more regulated procedural model based on summary conviction is easing out the looser, more diffuse mode of social control exemplified by the bind-over. Such a movement may also in part explain the increase in provision of the summary, magisterial, alternative to jury trial. Juries were less predictable than Justices, or at least it was so thought in some quarters, and no juries, as we shall see, were considered less predictable than those in Wales.

Yet a problem of relying on Justice of the Peace, whose active numbers were always only a proportion of those contained within the nominal commissions, was that they were not uniformly distributed within the counties. In some places towns had increased in size and importance, whilst the country gentlemen of the bench remained resident at a considerable distance from them. In Anglesey, for example, a bench which was to be split by personal and political divisions in the 1840s, there was concern that the area around the expanding port of Holyhead was ill-served by the county's magistracy. The distance between the Justices and the public they were charged with supervising might be not only a geographical one but also a social one, not simply in obvious class terms but also cutting across religious affiliations and the agricultural/commercial divide.[72] In Welsh-speaking areas, knowledge of the language was still regarded as a considerable advantage for a Justice of the Peace, though one magistrate observed that "even without knowing Welsh I should be of much use for Parish business ... I must get Burns [sic] Justice and read a bit".[73] Such a relaxed attitude towards legal knowledge is perhaps not unreasonable, but it may explain deviations from or uncertainty concerning the law which sometimes mark the judgments of Justices of the Peace.[74] Nonetheless, a fluency in Welsh was not guaranteed as the century wore on. Ellis Jones concludes his investigation by stating:

> the fact remains that the overwhelming majority at the end of the nine-teenth century were not Welsh speakers, and the treatment of Welsh speakers at petty and Quarter Sessions throughout the century depended largely on the predilections and whims of individual magistrates.[75]

Linguistic issues might also arise with trials before juries, the problem there being an inability of the members of the jury to understand English. In this, of course, their inadequacy might be shared with the defendant who could find him or herself on trial, even in capital cases, in a language they did not understand. Similarly, witnesses in the trial might need to testify in Welsh and, when one was threatened with a loss of expenses for wanting to answer in that language in a rape case at Monmouthshire Assizes in 1851, the matter was raised in the House of Lords. This linguistic discomfort seems certainly, as contemporary observers like the barrister Lewis Morris recognized, to have fed into a representation of the Welsh jury as unreliable or even contrary.[76] Although there are statistics, admittedly flawed, for the use of Welsh generally by the population in the latter part of the century[77], there is no statistical evidence to indicate how frequent, how localized and how persistent the problem of largely monoglot juries was within Wales. It is clear, however, that in counties like Cardiganshire and Carmarthenshire it was not an insignif-icant matter. The results could also be a source of some amusement to Eng-lish judges, if we are to believe the letter sent by James Fitzjames Stephen, writing to a friend from his first Circuit in Wales:

> When Bramwell was judging here, one of the counsel who spoke to the jury in Welsh told them they must not mind what the old man in the red gown told them, he was only a Saxon oppressor, come to trouble the good old Welsh laws and customs![78]

Yet I suspect that language was not the only factor in the perception of the Welsh jury (which had a lower property qualification at Quarter Sessions level than its English equivalent under the 1825 Juries Act, a differential reversed in 1870) as rather "cavalier". That their findings did not always seem war-ranted by the evidence presented might imply also the survival of a rather older conception of jury responsibility which we have discussed at length earlier. Juries continued to judge the fate of a defendant on a broader con-ception of his merits than in relation to his particular offence, and on the issue not of what had been done, but whether it deserved juridical (and it should be remembered that this was not the only form available) punishment.[79] Welsh-speaking defendants in criminal cases were afforded, although there was, as far as I know, no statutory entitlement to, the services of an interpreter, although the abilities of those acting in that capacity were not always unimpeachable. However a move in 1875 to set up a Select Committee on the desirability of providing official, state-funded interpreters came to nothing.[80]

One of the most momentous developments within the criminal justice system of the nineteenth century within the British Isles as a whole was the creation and spread of the "New Police", which replaced the earlier system of watchmen and parish constables.[81] In Wales the development of the forces, assisted in some areas by pressure as a result of the popular disturbances discussed earlier in this chapter, began early and had, I will suggest, particular and important effects.[82] That is not to say that such effects were necessarily immediate or dramatic. The Municipal Corporations Act which required the establishment of forces within the boroughs seems, in the short term, simply to have allowed the substitution of one set of political placemen by another. This seems true, at any rate, of Carmarthen, a town the governance of which had been lambasted in the report leading to that Act.[83] Nor should we believe that the task of *prosecution* of offenders was assumed wholesale by the new forces once they had been established. It is true that many offences related to public disorder or to regulatory matters were taken over by the police, but major crime long rested on prosecution by interested parties, a fact dramatically evidenced in the Jacob case discussed above, where none had come forward. Indeed it is easy to ignore the mundane and undramatic nature of much early police work: serving bastardy orders or supervising regulations concerning animals took up much of the time of rural officers. Despite the increasing prominence of a detective function, particularly in the Metropolitan force, in the later part of the century, much of the criminal function of the police remained, as it was originally conceived, preventative. Officers patrolled fairs, or attended at the paydays of mines, or, even before the Habitual Criminals Act of 1869 placed this function on a statutory basis, to keep suspected individuals under observation. A Montgomeryshire constable recorded in his journal in 1844 in relation to his looking over the house of a suspected family, "My intention was to keep fear on them".[84]

Such observation of working-class life by the police was not always welcome. There was, as elsewhere, some opposition to the creation of the new forces, although this might arise primarily on the grounds of their cost. Amongst boroughs, Kidwelly held out against the County Force for a while, and posters in Aberystwyth proclaimed the town's proposed new force unnecessary.[85] There were moves in Denbighshire in 1842 to abolish the force which had been created only 2 years earlier, whilst, even when the police were well established, the Home Office might have to fight attempts to diminish the status of the service. In 1873 Radnorshire attempted to make savings in the cost of its police, asserting that "crime is singularly trivial both in number and the character of the cases".[86] Interestingly, as the century wore on, pressure was maintained on the performance of the police by local newspapers, which had fast become a major source of information and concern about crime. Robinson's study of the role of the *Cardiff Times* in the 1880s shows the paper not only attempting to set the agenda on tackling criminality in the city but also criticizing the police for their efforts. The editor of the *Aberystwyth Advertiser* launched a similar attack on the shortcomings of his local force in 1897.[87]

By then, of course, the police were well entrenched, and it would be wise not to give the impression that hostility to the forces was throughout the only response: many individuals and officials welcomed their introduction and development, whilst many simply got used to their presence as a fact of life. It was, I suggest, a slightly different way of life as a result of their introduction. It is perhaps reading too much into the words of Hettie Davies of Cardiganshire in 1894, "Plismon yn wir, be mae nhw'n feddwl ydym ni?" ("A policeman indeed, what do they take us for?")[88] to suggest that the slight perceived was not only on the character of the people but also on their capacity to police themselves without outside intervention. Nonetheless, the "external" agency of the police may have contributed to a notable shift in concept of peacekeeping. The constabularies, of course, were locally run and locally recruited, and facility in the Welsh language was considered important in some forces even at the level of Chief Constable.[89] Nonetheless the individual forces formed part of a greater systemic whole with their English equivalents, and through the oversight of the Inspectorate of Constabulary and the Home Office it was a system which in some respects transcended the local experience.[90] The communications which developed between different forces and the often remarkable artefacts they produced such as the photograph albums held at Ruthin and Aberystwyth and, after 1869, in the central Register of Habitual Offenders in London, evidence a most important development.[91] Alongside such other nineteenth-century reforms such as those relating to the Poor Law, to provision of lunatic asylums and to prison administration, they demonstrate a much tighter, bureaucratically controlled "national" (i.e. England and Wales) approach to social problems. In such an atmosphere Welsh "exceptionalism", though it might still exist, was less robust. It is interesting to note, in this context, a comment by the Chief Constable of Cardiganshire at the beginning of the twentieth century that the benefits of the police included the disappearance of "the carrying of effigies (cefyllau pren)", whilst the mayor of Caernarfon reported in 1861 that "people are now afraid to compromise felonies as they formerly did".[92] It would seem that traditional methods of dispute settlement were in decline for a variety of reasons, not only demographic but also related to the systemic intervention of the Victorian state.

The same may be said of the creation of a national prison service in the nineteenth century. Originally the operation and funding of prisons was a local affair, dependent on individual counties and boroughs. Prison moved to the head of the Victorian penal agenda, replacing capital and corporal punishment as the punitive response to the majority of crimes for which pecuniary or other lesser penalties were deemed inadequate. Imprisonment also eventually completely replaced transportation, abolished as a punishment in 1857. As part of this shift, central intervention in and regulation of imprisonment became more marked. The construction of national penitentiaries in England provided a hub around which the local gaols were theoretically located, whilst the latter were increasingly subject to statutory intervention of their own. This regulation was at first permissive, but was later afforced by the use of the Prison Inspectorate, culminating eventually in nationalization of the prison system by an Act of 1877. As I have argued at length elsewhere, it would be wrong to see Welsh prisons as simply reacting passively to such changes; local pride, local economy and specific issues such as the linguistic and religious particularities of much of the Welsh prison population ensured that the Victorian goal of systemic uniformity was not to be easily achieved.[93] Language issues were raised in Welsh establishments, although possibly with an eye principally to causing political embarrassment, from the Quarter Sessions in Cardiganshire in 1893. The Home Secretary refused to interfere in the matter.[94] Prison Inspectors could find themselves surprised by affairs as they were conducted in remoter counties. Sometimes, as at Carmarthen or Montgomery at mid-century, understaffing defeated a national policy which sought to impose silent association within gaols, and Carmarthen's building of a non-cellular women's prison, employing instead the older model of communal accommodation as late as 1857, drew the Inspector's wrath.[95] More seriously, the conduct of the gaoler and Visiting Justices (the County body responsible for overseeing the County Gaol) in Caernarfon resulted in considerable scandal. A report into allegations of ill-treatment of prisoners and other issues such as his permitting cock-fighting in the gaol concluded that the gaoler was:

> not of strictly sober habits; that he has treated with cruelty some of the prisoners committed to his charge, that he has exercised his authority in a vexatious and unlawful manner, that he has permitted, if not promoted, great irregularities in the prison; that he is in the habit of cursing and swearing

and recommended his removal, a recommendation which, notwithstanding such a catalogue of default, the independent local magistracy were reluctant to implement.[96]

Yet a problem within the prison system which made itself felt less directly was not misfeasance, but nonfeasance. Poorer, outlying counties such as Cardiganshire responded to the mandatory provisions of the 1865 Prison Act which imposed uniformity of cell and labour provision on all county gaols in the same way as it had earlier responded to the County Asylums Act. It played for time, sitting tight until its gaol was closed at nationalization, its prisoners being removed, with those of Pembrokeshire, to the recently expensively rebuilt gaol at Carmarthen.[97] Such consolidation was not without problems of its own, however, for increasing distances from an offender's home to the place

Figure 4.2 Interior of Montgomery Gaol, *c.* 1875.
Courtesy Powysland Museum.

of confinement might cause hardship. It was apparently without any sense of irony that the Cardiganshire bench itself made representations to the Home Secretary in 1893 asking for a place of detention to be established within the county for prisoners held on remand.[98] The concentration of prison provision after the system became a national one would continue to cause difficulty for prisoners and their families from less populated areas of Wales into the next century and beyond.

It was a recognition of the limitations of incarceration as well as a change in attitude towards specific classes of offenders which saw an expansion in the provision of more specialist institutions within the nineteenth century. Juvenile crime was felt to merit, at least in part, special provision, but Reformatories did not come early to Wales, though the Carmarthenshire Bench had voiced the need for one as early as 1847. The first was opened at Howdref Ganol near Neath in 1858, another, Little Mill, opened near Pontypool in the same year. North Wales did not get such provision until a Catholic reformatory opened in Mold in 1899. Some Welsh juveniles, including the girls, were sent outside the country. Such was the fate, for example, of 15-year-old sailor David Jones, convicted of the rape of a child in Llanilar, who was sent to the reformatory ship Akbar lying off Liverpool. Industrial schools, designed for juveniles considered less deeply involved in criminality than those for whom reformatory schools were designed, also made use of ships, the first of these in Britain, the *Havannah*, being opened in Cardiff in 1861. This event gratified no less a campaigner for reformatory discipline than the celebrated Mary Carpenter, who declared (perhaps ambiguously!) "If such a school is needed anywhere in the world it certainly is at Cardiff". A second such ship, the *Clio*, opened off Bangor in 1877, complementing reformatory schools based in towns in Wales.[99] The Victorian enthusiasm for institutionalization also embraced prostitutes, for whom a "House of Refuge for Distressed Women" was opened at Llandaff in 1862, and provision was also made at Cardiff and Swansea for vagrants.[100] These latter, of course were also to be found passing through the workhouse system established under the 1834 Poor Law. The line between welfare provision and punishment was blurred in the operation of these workhouses, which also performed a role, generally overlooked, in the "secondary institutionalization" of the dependents of incarcerated criminals. Bread-winners sentenced to terms of imprisonment might also see their families removed to the workhouse, an institution whose difference to the prison was not always appreciated by its inmates. Asylum provision also merits a mention here, as increasingly throughout the nineteenth century "alienists" (i.e. those claiming expertise in mental disorder) and lawyers engaged directly with the problems of dealing with mentally abnormal offenders. Welsh asylums were established, albeit in some instances belatedly, which would receive such offenders as well as non-criminal patients. Such an offender was the 27-year-old David Jenkins, who gazes out quizzically at the photographer in the Carmarthen Felons' Register, but the asylum itself was not invariably a place of safety for those confined within it, as a number of allegations of abuse in the 1860s and '70s from Carmarthen's Joint Counties Lunatic Asylum make clear.[101]

It is worth pausing for a moment over the name of that institution. It took inmates from Cardiganshire and Pembrokeshire as well as Carmarthenshire. Relatively poor counties found it financially difficult to meet their individual statutory obligations in this area, as we have seen was also the case with prison provision. The bureaucratic response was to look beyond the traditional boundaries of the county and to consolidate institutional provision. This mentality may be taken as symbolic of one aspect of an increasingly important trend within the nineteenth century. Crime and punishment become matters of national concern, by which is meant in this instance the nation as comprising England and Wales, rather than simply matters for local administration. We have seen in this chapter that, whilst popular sentiment and custom might still prove to be distinctive and important in attitudes towards criminality within Wales, wider developments, not only in relation to demographic and economic change but also in the bureaucratic pull of Home Office control were operating to erode the significance of traditional practices and boundaries. In the next chapter we must consider whether there is, in the twentieth century, still any point in pursuing a specifically Welsh dimension in crime and the response to it.

Notes

1 For figures and discussion, see Davies, *History of Wales*, pp. 319ff., 398ff. (though note Davies's time frames extend outside the nineteenth century, narrowly defined), D.J.V. Jones, *Before Rebecca*, p. 5. For Carmarthenshire, see R. Davies, *Secret Sins: Sex Violence and Society in Carmarthenshire 1870–1920* (Cardiff: University of Wales Press, 1996) Ch. 1; for urbanization, N. Evans, "The urbanization of Welsh society" in T. Herbert and G.E. Jones (eds) *People and Protest: Wales 1815–1850* (Cardiff: University of Wales Press, 1988) p. 7.

2 For the "penal revolution", see Ireland, *Want of Order*, Introduction.

3 See R.W. Ireland, "Putting oneself on whose country?" p. 63 at p. 65.

4 K. Jones, *Newcastle Emlyn Miscellany 1810–1960* (Newcastle Emlyn: Summerhill Press, 2012) p. 62. The device is termed "the stocks" but clearly the wrists could be fastened. The pillory was formally abolished in 1837. The date hazarded in Jones's source is "around 1872", and the corroborated witness statements are entirely reliable, but I find no conviction for Foster in that year, though there is one in the previous year which, unsurprisingly, omits the gothic and presumably illegal details, see *Cardigan and Tivy-Side Advertiser*, 23 June 1871.

5 Carmarthen Record Office, hereafter C.R.O., QS Box 16.

6 D. Parry-Jones, *Welsh Country Upbringing* (2nd edn, London: B.T. Batsford, 1949) p. 32.

7 For the terms and rhetoric, see Ireland, "A second Ireland" esp. notes 7 and 8 at p. 254 for references. The verse is apparently first attested in 1780. Interestingly it was discussed in *The Cambrian News*, 27 September 1872.

8 For more on this issue, see Jones, *Crime in Wales*, Ch. 2.

9 *Report of the Royal Commission to Inquire into the Means of Education Available in Wales* (First Part) 1847 [870] xxvii, p. 304.

10 See K. Strange, *Merthyr Tydfil: Iron Metropolis* (Stroud: The History Press, 2005) p. 110. For crime in Merthyr generally, see Chs 6 and 7 and the same author's "In search of the celestial empire: crime in Merthyr, 1830–60" *Llafur* 3 (1980): 44.

11 Parry-Jones, *Welsh Country Upbringing*, p. 134. See also the letter from Edward Head in relation to the "Hill population of Monmouthshire and Glamorganshire", a "penal settlement as well as a prosperous manufacturing district. Whenever a man runs away from his family or commits any depredation in … the adjoining counties the answer to any enquiry is, 'he has gone to the Hills'", in D.J.V. Jones, "Scotch cattle and Chartism" in T. Herbert and G.E. Jones (eds) *People and Protest*, pp. 150–151. Note, too, the opinion of a commentator of 1804: "The simplicity, sincerity and disinterestedness of the peasant is lost in the mercenary cunning or extortion of the mechanic", Jones, *Before Rebecca*, p. 202.

12 See R.W. Ireland, "A second Ireland" p. 239, "Whose country" p. 67, D.J.V. Jones, *Crime in Nineteenth-Century Wales*, Ch. 1. This latter text is a groundbreaking study in relation to the subject of this chapter and in particular in its analysis of official statistics.

13 S.H. Jones-Parry, "Crime in Wales" *The Red Dragon* III (1888): 522.

14 See Ireland, "A second Ireland". For the Irish and the navvies in Monmouthshire records, see T. Hopkins, "Quarter sessions and the justice of the peace in Monmouthshire" *The Monmouthshire Antiquary* (2013) xxix: 47 at p. 58.

15 For discussion, see Parry, *Great Sessions*, pp. xxiii *et seq.*, esp. pp. xxxix, xxxvii, W. Cornish, S. Anderson, R. Cocks, M. Lobban, P. Polden, K. Smith, *The Oxford History of the Laws of England Vol. xi 1820–1914: English* [sic] *Legal System* pp. 631–636.

16 For the argument, see Ireland, "Whose country" pp. 78–80.

17 D.J.V. Jones, "A dead loss to the community: the criminal vagrant in mid-nineteenth-century Wales"*Welsh History Review* 8 (1977): 312 at p. 313, P. O'Leary, *Immigration and Integration: The Irish in Wales, 1798–1922* (Cardiff: University of Wales Press, 2000) p. 185.

18 For vagrancy, see ibid., W. Griffith, *Power, Politics and County Government in Wales: Anglesey 1780–1914* (Llangefni: Anglesey Antiquarian Society, 2006) pp. 171–172, Davies, *Law and Disorder*, pp. 102–103; Davies, *Secret Sins*, p. 58–61, Strange, "Celestial empire" pp. 68–69; Ireland, *Want of Order*, pp. 147, 159–160, 166–667.

19 For the Penmaenmawr, see *The Preston Guardian*, 30 May 1846, T. Coleman, *The Railway Navvies* (London: Penguin, 1972) p. 24; for Ferryside and the question of policing, see R.W. Ireland, "'An increasing mass of heathens in the bosom of a Christian land': the railway and crime in the nineteenth century" *Continuity and Change* 12 (1997): 55, which also discusses the impact of the railway on crime in Carmarthenshire more generally.

20 Note Davies, *Secret Sins*, at p. 162 for rural prostitution.

21 For Newport and Cardiff, see T. Jukes, "'Mary the Cripple': the Yarwood family's life of crime and vice in Victorian South Wales" *Gwent Local History* 111 (2012): 18; for Wrexham, F. Clements, "Female crime and punishment in nineteenth century Denbighshire" *Denbighshire Historical Society Transactions* 60 (2012): 95 at 98; for the information concerning Welshpool, I am indebted to Rachael Jones.

22 Strange, *Merthyr Tydfil*, pp. 109–110.

23 *Carmarthen Journal*, 26 December 1861; and see also 2 January 1852 for an investigation of the matter. *P.C. Williams's Diary 1859–60*, C.R.O. Museum 112.

24 Rose, *Pembroke People*, pp. 347–352.

25 See Jones, *Before Rebecca*, Ch. 2, Davies, *History of Wales*, p. 356.

26 Jones, *Before Rebecca*, Ch. 2; T. Herbert and G.E. Jones (eds), *People and Protest: Wales 1815–1850*.

27 Ibid., Ch. 3, Jones, "Scotch cattle and Chartism", R.E. Jones, "Symbol, ritual and popular protest in early nineteenth-century Wales: the Scotch cattle rebranded", *Welsh History Review* 26 (2012): p. 34.

28 See Davies, *History* pp. 366–367, Jones, *Before Rebecca*, Ch. 6 and, for the trial, N. Cooke "*The King v Richard Lewis and Lewis Lewis* (Cardiff, 13 July 1831): the trial of Dic Penderyn" in T. Watkin (ed.) *The Trial of Dic Penderyn and Other Essays* (Cardiff: Welsh Legal History Society, 2002) p. 110.

29 See Jones, "Scotch cattle and Chartism", M. Chase, "Rethinking Welsh Chartism" and O. Ashton, "Chartism in Llanidloes: the riot of 1839 revisited" both *Llafur* 10 (2010): 39 and 76.

30 *Prison Inspector's Fifth Report*, 1840 [255] xxv.721.

31 Jones, "Scotch cattle and Chartism" p. 148; see also his *The Last Rising: The Newport Insurrection of 1839* (Cardiff: University of Wales Press, 1985) and I. Wilks, *South Wales and the Rising of 1839* (Llandysul: Gomer Press, 1989) for more detailed analyses.

32 For the response, see Jones, *Last Rising*, Ch. 6.

33 "And they blessed Rebekah, and said unto her, Thou art our sister, be thou the mother of thousands of millions, and let thy seed possess the gates of those which hate them" (Genesis 24: 60). The "inversion" of female dress is addressed in Jones "Symbol, ritual and popular protest". For myself, though I admit the importance of a ritualized, theatrical display, I am rather more prosaic than some: poor farmers had little clothing in which they might disguise themselves. For the riots more generally, see D.J.V. Jones, *Rebecca's Children* (Cardiff: University of Wales Press, 1989), and "Rebecca, crime and policing: a turning point in nineteenth-century attitudes" *Transactions of the Honourable Society of*

Cymmrodorion (1990): 99; D. Howell, "The Rebecca Riots" in Herbert and Jones (eds), *People and Protest*, p. 113, P. Molloy, *And They Blessed Rebecca* (Llandysul: Gomer Press, 1983), D. Williams, *The Rebecca Riots* (Cardiff: University of Wales Press, 1955).

34 Such a call for outside assistance from the police (as opposed to the military) was not unprecedented: as early as 1800 the Mayor of Haverfordwest had requested the intervention of the Bow Street Runners; see Jones, *Before Rebecca*, p. 178.

35 Jones, "Rebecca, crime and policing" p. 105, Ireland, "A second Ireland" p. 242. Successive Governors of Carmarthen Gaol were formerly Metropolitan Officers.

36 For my own discussion of these Reports, see Ireland, *Want of Order*, pp. 56–66.

37 M. Jones, "Rural and industrial protest in North Wales" in Herbert and Jones (eds) *People and Protest*. For the fishery disputes, see K. Parker, *Parties, Polls and Riots: Politics in Nineteenth-Century Radnorshire* (Woonton Almeley: Logaston Press, 2008) Ch. 8.

38 See J. Parry, "The Tredegar anti-Irish riots of 1882 in *Llafur* (1983) 3: 20. It was not only the Irish, of course, who were seen as a threat to "local" jobs. A major riot in Mold in 1869, in which four were killed when troops fired on the crowd, involved hostility to incomer miners and was provoked by the attempt to remove a colliery manager from Durham. In the aftermath the Governor of Flint Gaol, fearing attack, telegraphed the Secretary of State for "twelve Snider carbines and 760 rounds of ammunition". See Clwyd R.O., *The Mold Riots* (Clwyd: Clwyd Record Office, 1991) p. 8. The employment of English mine-agents, gamekeepers, and, in the Tithe Wars, bailiffs and auctioneers was often used as a deliberate policy to preserve a distance from, and an independence of, those with whom they dealt.

39 Jones, "Rural and industrial protest" p. 166, T. Jones, *Rioting in North East Wales*, p. 65.

40 Jones, *Rioting in North East Wales, loc. cit.*

41 See generally for the background, Watkin, *Legal History*, p. 178. Jones "Rural and industrial protest" pp. 175, 189.

42 *Cardigan and Tivy-Side Advertiser*, 19, 26 May 1893, 7 July 1893. For the role of the crowd inside and outside the courtroom generally in nineteenth-century Wales see Ireland, "A second Ireland" pp. 247–252.

43 *Cardigan and Tivy-Side Advertiser*, 23 June 1893.

44 See Ireland, *Want of Order*, pp. 75–77 and note there, too, that other members of the community might involve themselves in the process.

45 Parry-Jones, *Welsh Country Upbringing*, p. 32. It is possible that the payment was merely to ensure silence, but I think this the least likely interpretation of the incident.

46 Per D.J. Williams, noted and discussed in Ireland, "A second Ireland" p. 246. Note also a description of clergymen of the established church in the 1850s as "spiritual constables or police in black instead of blue clothes", H.C. Birch, *The History of Policing in North Wales* (Pwllheli: Gwasg Correg Gwalch, 2008) p. 56.

47 For the subject generally, see Ireland, *Want of Order*, pp. 68–72, R. Jones, "Popular culture, policing and the disappearance of the Ceffyl Pren in Cardiganshire *c.* 1837–1850" *Ceredigion* (1998–1999) 11: 19. I would add the observation that the symbolism seems to invert the festive visitations of the traditional Welsh "good" horse, the Mari Llywd (known in Carmarthenshire as the "Pen Ceffyl" according to R. Hutton, *Stations of the Sun: A History of the Ritual Year in Britain* (Oxford: Oxford University Press, 2001) p. 84).

48 Ireland, *Want of Order*, pp. 71–72.

49 S. Dubé (ed.), *My Failings and Imperfections: The Diary of Rees Thomas of Dôl-llan, 1860–1862* (Llandybie: Carmarthenshire Antiquarian Society, 2011) pp. 58, 59, 61.

50 The case is discussed in R. Jones, "Popular culture"; the Assize records are at The National Archives (TNA) Assi 72/1. The focus of this riding, a man called Gordon, had informed against someone for cutting timber. Interestingly in 1857 the police intervened to prevent a *ceffyl pren* in the small Cardiganshire settlement of Llangeitho at which some 2,000 people were reported to be in attendance; see *Diary of PC Phillip Davies (1857–1860)*, 31 March 1857, Ceredigion Archives ADX/1405.

51 R. Jones, "Women, community and collective action: the Ceffyl Pren tradition" in A. John (ed.) *Our Mothers' Land: Chapters in Welsh Women's History 1830–1939* (Cardiff: University of Wales Press, 1991) p. 17. For details of a late example, see, e.g., *The Western Mail*, 23 January 1893. I am grateful to Siti Jamil for this reference.

52 Jones, *Crime in Wales*, pp. 12–13; see also, e.g., P. Molloy, *A Shilling for Carmarthen* (Fishguard: Gomer Press, 1991) Ch. 10; R.M. Jones, *The North Wales Quarrymen 1874–1922* (Cardiff: University of Wales Press, 1982) pp. 46–47.

53 Ibid., p. 93, pp. 89–93.

54 See Ireland, *Want of Order*, pp. 101–104. Note the remarks from the Carmarthen bench to Frederick Jones, "as it was his first offence the Bench thought he had been sufficiently punished by having been shut up in the Station-house during the preceding night" *Carmarthen Journal*, 3 January 1851.

55 *Cardigan and Tivy-Side Advertiser*, 11 February 1870.

56 Davies *Secret Sins*, pp. 116–122. As to the licensing sessions themselves I am much taken by a diary entry reproduced in M.G.R. Morris (ed.), *Romilly's Visits to Wales 1827–1854* (Llandysul: Gomer Press, 1998) p. 107 for 31 August 1854 relating to a sitting in Narberth: "George sat on the bench with two other magistrates (Dr Thomas – a great liar – and Mr Buckler, an intelligent Irish clergyman) to license publicans. On these licensing occasions the magistrates are provided with a green bottle of sherry and a bag of biscuits".

57 See Jones, *Crime in Wales*, Ch. 3. For an interesting instance of a form of violence formerly considered socially acceptable, see K. Jones, *Alas! Poor Heslop: the Last Fatal Duel in Wales* (Cardigan: Summerhill Press, 2007).

58 See R.W. Ireland and R.I. Ireland (eds), *The Carmarthen Gaoler's Journal 1845–50 Part One* (Bangor: Welsh Legal History Society, 2010) pp. 180–181.

59 Molloy, *Shilling for Carmarthen*, p. 148.

60 I. Davies, "The last time 'justice' was seen to be done: the fate of Matthew Francis of Newport" *Gwent Local History* 106 (2009): 36 *et seq.*; see also Davies, *Law and Disorder*, p. 110.

61 For this case and a discussion of the issues within this paragraph, see Ireland, "A second Ireland" pp. 247–252.

62 For the argument and illustrations, see Ireland, "Perhaps my mother", "Whose country", both *passim*, and *Want of Order*, p. 76. For discussion generally, see Jones, *Crime in Wales*, pp. 76 (where an overall 40 per cent conviction rate for infanticide seems surprising after the Carmarthenshire evidence) 79–81, 82–84, Davies, *Secret Sins*, pp. 171, 173–175, Clements, "Female crime" p. 100. For infanticide figures from England, see J. Flanders, *The Invention of Murder* (London: Harper Press, 2011) p. 225. Davies remarks on the approaches to the Grand Jury to bring indictments for lesser offences in sexual offences. See the case of Henry Davies, taken for "a more serious offence", almost certainly rape, indicted for indecent assault, prosecuted for common assault, *Carmarthen Journal*, 10 January 1851.

63 For an analysis of the case, see R.W. Ireland, "Sanctity, superstition and the death of Sarah Jacob" in A. Musson and C. Stebbings (eds) *Making Legal History: Approaches and Methodologies* (Cambridge: Cambridge University Press, 2012) p. 284.

64 See S. White, "A burial ahead of its time: the *Crookenden Burial Case* and the sanctioning of cremation in England and Wales" in Watkin (ed.) *Trial of Dic Penderyn*, p. 151.

65 Jones, *Crime in Wales*, Ch. 4. For case studies from Breconshire, see Davies, *Law and Disorder*, Ch. 3.

66 Ireland, "Increasing mass of heathens"; for drovers and the railways, see R.J. Moore-Colyer, *Welsh Cattle Drovers: Agriculture and the Welsh Cattle Trade before and during the Nineteenth Century* (Ashbourne: University of Wales Press, 2002) pp. 108–113, for a fatal attack on a butter merchant returning from the industrial South, see Davies, *Law and Disorder*, pp. 110–121. Davies also gives a case of theft by thimblemen at Brecon Fair in 1833 (pp. 138–140), possibly the same gang who were removed from Carmarthen Fair in the same year: see Ireland, *Want of Order*, p. 92. I am struck by a newspaper description of a suspected pickpocket "a cadaverous hunchback with a restless eye and long arms and fingers" *Carmarthen Journal*, 3 December 1853.

67 Jones, *Crime in Wales*, pp. 126–127.

68 See, Jones, *Crime in Wales*, pp. 128–133 and compare the Wye fisheries cases discussed above, Davies, *Secret Sins*, pp. 128–131. For the magistrates' role, see, e.g., the cases reported in the *Carmarthen Journal*, 18 February 1853. Another property addressed by Jones (pp. 133–137) is criminal damage, to buildings and to animals. On occasion such damage, or intimations of such damage, might be accompanied by threatening letters to which the Welsh, according to Lord Penrhyn, were "addicted" (Jones, "Rural and industrial protest" p. 172). For an interesting case, with an interesting outcome, and reference to the Royal Commission, see R. Jones, "Three legal cases from the history of the Gregynog estate" in T.G. Watkin (ed.) *The Carno Poisonings and Other Essays* (Bangor: Welsh Legal History Society, 2013) p. 121 at pp. 123–126.

69 Jones, *Crime in Wales*, Ch. 5; Ireland, *Want of Order*, pp. 85–86.

70 See, e.g., Coal Mines Regulation Act 1887, Factory and Workshop Act 1891, M. Ellis Jones, "'The confusion of Babel'? The Welsh language, law courts and legislation in the nineteenth century" in G. Jenkins (ed.) *The Welsh Language and its Social Domains 1801–1911* (Cardiff: University of Wales Press, 2000) p. 587 at p. 605.

71 Watson, "Women, crime and justice" p. 22.

72 W. Griffith, *Power, Politics and County Government in Wales*, Chs 3 and 4.

73 Griffith, *Power, Politics*, p. 65.

74 Ireland, *Want of Order*, p. 77.

75 See Ellis Jones, "Confusion of Babel" pp. 607 ff.

76 For such a perception, which was evidenced before the Select Committee on the Administration of Justice in Wales 1817–21 and before the Commissioners on the Superior Courts of Common Law in 1829, see Ireland, "Whose country" *passim*. The quote from Morris is at p. 76. See also Jones, *Crime in Wales*, p. 219 *et seq*. Jones's finding that acquittal rates were "a little higher than those in England" is interesting, but it is impossible, of course, to determine whether different verdicts would have been returned in the same case in the different countries.

77 See D. Jones, *Statistical Evidence relating to the Welsh Language 1801–1911* (Cardiff: University of Wales Press, 1998).

78 Quoted in White, "Burial ahead of its time" p. 168.

79 For a more detailed discussion, see Ireland, "Whose country" *passim*, *Want of Order*, pp. 72–74.

80 For interpreters, see, e.g., *Carmarthen Journal*, 21 July 1865, a perjury trial, though the translator complained of had acted in the County Court in this case. In one remarkable instance the presence of an Irish-speaking defendant led to

the swearing in of a member of the County Police as a translator and "as many of the jury could not comprehend English, a Welsh interpreter was sworn, and the court then presented the singular spectacle of a trial being conducted in three different languages" (*Carmarthen Journal*, 21 October 1853). Policemen could also be used as interpreters in arbitration, see, e.g., *Diary of P.C. Davies*, 23 March 1859 (*supra* note 50). Counsel themselves might have no Welsh; it was stated in 1871 that there were only two Welsh speakers at the North Wales bar (*Carmarthen Journal*, 24 November 1871). For the move for a Select Committee, see Ellis Jones, "Confusion of Babel" p. 615.

81   On which see generally, e.g., P. Rawlings, *Policing: A Short History* (Cullompton: Willan, 2002).

82   See generally Jones, *Crime in Wales*, pp. 201–216. For the establishment of particular forces, see Appendix 1.

83   See *First Report of the Commissioners on Municipal Corporations in England and Wales 1835* (438) xi for the report, P. Molloy, *A Shilling for Carmarthen*, Ch. 3 for the results.

84   Powys Digital History Project. For details of everyday policing in West Wales, see *Diary of PC Davies*, Ceredigion Archives ADX/1405, *Diaries of P.C. (later P.S.) Williams*, Carms Archives Mus.112. For the policing of habitual criminals, see Ireland, *Want of Good Order*, pp. 174–175. Constables might be privately hired for particular duties, and note the hiring of detectives from Liverpool to work undercover at fairs. Birch, *History of Policing*, pp. 77, 125.

85   J.F. Jones, "Kidwelly Borough Police Force" *The Carmarthenshire Antiquary* 4 (1963): 152, Parry, *Launched to Etenity*, p. 17 for the Aberystwyth poster, presumably produced in anticipation of the merger of the Borough with the County force in 1857.

86   Birch, *History of Policing*, Ch. 2, A. Page, "The Radnorshire Quarter Sessions, 1773–1873" *The Transactions of The Radnorshire Society* lxxx (2010): 83 at pp. 93–94.

87   See D. Robinson, "Crime, police and the provincial press: a study of Victorian Cardiff" *Welsh History Review* 25 (2011): 551, R.W. Ireland, "Caught on camera: Cardiganshire's criminal portraits in context" *Ceredigion* xv (2006) 11: 17–19, which also records an outburst from a local MP against the police from the Petty Sessions bench in 1907.

88   G. Williams, "The disenchantment of the world: innovation, crisis and change in Cardiganshire c 1880–1910" *Ceredigion* ix (1983): 303 at p. 313.

89   For the language and the police see Jones, *Crime in Wales*, p. 213, Birch, *History of Policing*, pp. 90–93, 147–154, Ellis Jones, "Confusion of Babel" p. 609, Strange, *Merthyr Tydfil*, p. 113.

90   Note, too, the importance of the police as gathering information on offences, particularly after 1857, as productive of the idea of crime, statistically measured, being constructed in national rather than local terms, on which see R.W. Ireland "Criminology, class and cricket: Raffles and real life" *Legal Studies* 33 (2013): 66.

91   NLW MS; see Ireland, "Caught on camera" and, for a discussion more generally of the role of photography in Wales in attempting to create a "national criminal", see my "The felon and the angel copier: criminal identity and the promise of photography in Victorian England and Wales" in L. Knafla (ed.) *Policing and War in Europe* (Westport, CT: Greenwood Press, 2002) p. 53.

92   *Cardiganshire Constabulary Chief Constable's Report*, 31 December 1900, p. 25; note also his observations on the pre-police situation: "a general impunity for crime committed, ... frequently accompanied by a kind of sickly sentimental satisfaction at the escape of offenders" (p. 12); for Caernarfon, see Jones, *Crime in Wales*, p. 210.

93   Ireland, *Want of Order passim*, especially Introduction. See also Jones, *Crime in Wales*, pp. 228 *et seq.*, and see Appendix 2 for further details.

94   See *Cambrian News*, 13 January 1893, 14 April 1893, *Manchester Guardian*, 1 July 1893. See also D.L. Jones, "A death at Borth in 1894: the capture, trial and execution of Thomas Richards" *Ceredigion* (2010) xvi: 11 at p. 36. The reply from the Home Secretary is recorded in the *Quarter Sessions Order Book* for the County at p. 200, which states that in 1892 seven of the 14 officers of Carmarthen Gaol spoke Welsh and there were only seven monoglot Welsh prisoners.

95   See for both gaols, for example *Prison Inspector's Twenty-Fourth Report* 1859 [2501 Sess. 1] xi. 169. For the daily operation of Carmarthen and the problems therein, see R.W. and R.I. Ireland, *The Carmarthen Gaoler's Journal 1845–50*.

96   *Report and Evidence Taken before Mr Russell, Inspector of Prisons, on the Late Inquiry Instituted into the Conduct of Mr George, Governor of the County Gaol of Carnarvon*, pp. 1843 (422) xliii. p. 12. S. McConville, *A History of English Prison Administration*, Vol I (London: Routledge and Kegan Paul, 1981) pp. 252–253.

97   Ireland *Want of Order*, pp. 122–123. Aberystwyth Borough Prison was one of the few closed specifically under the 1865 Act.

98   *Cambrian News*, 14 April 1893.

99   Jones, *Crime in Wales*, pp. 236–237, Ireland, *Want of Good Order*, pp. 175–181; P. Carradice, *Nautical Training Ships: An Illustrated History* (Stroud: Amberley Publishing, 2009) Chs 3 and 4. For the Jones case, see *Cardigan and Tivyside Advertiser*, 2 March 1877. For the rather different issue of infant children in gaol, see R.W. Ireland, "Confinement with hard labour: motherhood and penal practice in a Victorian gaol" *Welsh History Review* (1997) 18: 621.

100 Strange, "Celestial Empire" pp. 75–76, Jones, *Crime in Wales*, p. 235.

101 Ireland, *Want of Order*, pp. 216–219, Davies, *Secret Sins*, p. 95, *Carmarthen Felons' Register* CRO Acc. 4916 no.1219. The Asylums Act of 1845 made provision compulsory in all counties, but the Joint Counties was not opened for another 20 years. Similar lack of enthusiasm led to delays in constructing the workhouses required under the 1834 Poor Law in places like Lampeter, Rhayader and Builth (on which latter, see Parker, *Parties, Polls and Riots*, p. 146). Before the provision of asylums, the insane might be kept in prisons. In 1803, for example, a lunatic was being kept in chains in Montgomery, before a transfer to Bedlam, having killed two men, one a fellow prisoner. Wetton and Wetton, *Montgomery*, pp. 123–124. See also R.W. Ireland, "Eugene Buckley and the diagnosis of insanity in the early Victorian prison" *Llafur* (1993) 6: 5.

5 The twentieth century

Radicalism, drugs and sheep

David Jones concludes his impressive study of crime and policing in South Wales in the twentieth century by stating that, subject to some few exceptions, "there was not a permanently and distinctly Welsh character to the delinquency described in this book".[1] To an extent, such a conclusion will not come as a surprise to readers of the present volume, for we have seen that the staples of criminal behaviour noted here, drunkenness, petty theft, brawling, are not of a sort to be strictly confined within national boundaries. More often we have seen that it is the response to wrongdoing, the avoidance of official procedures and the desire to insinuate flexibility within them when they are invoked which have been notable Welsh characteristics in earlier chapters. Yet the feeling remains upon reviewing the criminal history of the last century that the Welsh experience is rather less distinctive, as Jones suggests, than was the case earlier. Such a feeling is resistant to statistical proof, for though statistics exist in abundance, they resist simple interpretation in the face of complex questions. Is the major increase in recorded crime witnessed, particularly in South Wales and particularly after the Second World War, simply indicative of an increase in crime itself, or is it a result of a greater willingness to report or record crime? Such a question is an overly familiar one to the criminologist. Yet, if we pull back further and try to explain the reasons which produce increases in any or all of those variables, and which further do so specifically in relation to Welsh history and experience, we find no sure answers but only hypotheses. Does urbanization explain the change, or the associated decline in traditional village community norms? A lessening of the controlling power of religion? Are an increase in communication, physical and otherwise, and a variation in the language in which that communication takes place factors in making elements of a culture less distinctive? Is simple familiarity with the structures and agencies of the state an explanation for an increased invocation of them? Other historians of Wales, better than I and with minds less focused on the specifics of criminality, will have much to say on the complexities of these issues.[2] Yet, in what follows, I will at times advert to such ideas, though never with confidence that I will provide a complete, or even a compelling, explanation.

Perhaps, however, in an attempt to atone for such shortcomings I might begin with three episodes which have made me smile, but which will, if considered more seriously raise questions about the vectors for, and resistances to, such change. The first appears in a 1960s television film, now held at the National Screen and Sound Archive of Wales in Aberystwyth. Detailing the instruction given to new Glamorgan police recruits from the Bridgend training centre, it includes footage of a "speech therapy" class, ostensibly designed to make officers more efficient in communication by the expedient of suppressing their natural accents. Quite how the clipped instructress's attempt to get one trainee to pronounce a rather plummy "rheaally" rather than his own "reelly" would assist conversation with Valleys' villains is not explained, but the desire to promote uniformity, as well as to add a marker of class difference, is interesting.[3] The second example refers to an element within the legal system which has been mentioned often in the preceding chapters. When Roderick Bowen QC welcomed Lord Chief Justice Parker to his first Welsh Assize, he vouchsafed, "You are about to meet a Welsh jury for the first time. Beware. Welsh juries are against sin – but not dogmatically so".[4] Finally, I recall a visit to a pub in some remote rural fastness over 30 years ago. Displayed on the bar was a large notice which informed patrons that it was an offence to serve alcohol to persons under the age of 18, before adding that beer and cider would be served to those over 16 on condition that they were well behaved. Even fresh from the study of legal anthropology I found such an instance of "private law-making" astonishing! The persistence of older attitudes towards state law, as also the evidence of a change in those attitudes will be a concern of this chapter.

The overall picture of the rate of crime in Wales during the twentieth century is that it was marginally lower than in England, though levels in the south were higher than the Welsh norm and higher than in some parts of England. The rise in levels of recorded criminality across Wales was dramatic in the second half of the century. Even within the south, though, crime was not uniformly experienced; the long association of disorder with seaports continued to affect Cardiff and Swansea well into the century, whilst latterly the housing estates in the economically deprived valleys, hit by the loss of traditional industries, experienced particular problems.[5] The traditional Welsh trope that criminality was the work of "outsiders", though it was still occasionally heard, was not convincing, although that is not to say that it was entirely without foundation. An analysis of the development of the A55 in North Wales which was completed in 1994 concluded that there was a strong indication that "infrastructure development within a given area has a strong effect on the types, levels, and patterns of crime committed within that area" and that an increase of "professional" crime in North Wales had been facilitated by the ease of access to it.[6]

Out in the countryside things seemed initially to remain rather different; indeed, when Princess Christian visited Llanybydder in 1906, a sign welcomed her to the "Land of White Gloves", an appellation which might have seemed rather stranger in Cardiff.[7] The persistence of some "anomalous" social patterns was such that in the 1950s anthropologists were studying rural Welsh normative structures with interest. The remains of the tradition of popular penality still survived there, although, as we shall see, it survived too in the industrial south, where the *ceffyl pren* had mutated into the "whiteshirting" and ostracism of strikebreakers. In the rural north there was evidence of the traditional role of shaming practice in regulating irregular (although not criminal) sexual relationships. A.D. Rees reports of a group of youths intervening in the affairs of a middle-aged widow and a younger male: "To break up the association they congregated around the house of the widow every time the lad was there, stopping up the chimney and throwing dead vermin and other obnoxious objects in through the doors and windows".[8] In Emmet's rather later study, the proliferation of poaching as a form of "anti-officialdom" rather than for economic motives and the avoidance of the formal legal system, in criminal as well as civil causes, drew the anthropologist's attention. As to the settlement of disputes, it is noted that:

> informal methods such as friendly compromise, fear of public opinion, the need to co-operate and finally ostracism, keep most disputes between people out of court, and if not an actual substitute for English Justice, make English justice (costly as well as foreign) only as a final and extreme resort.[9]

These instances are cited to indicate not only that traditions which we have noted throughout this volume survive until very late in those communities where the social conditions which support them remain relatively unchanged. Their appearance in anthropological literature also reveals the wider paradigm change which makes them seem anomalous and worthy of specific study in the first place. It is certainly not my contention that in rural communities little changed in the twentieth century, for we shall see that it did. We must be aware, however, that the extent and timescale of that change was not uniform across Wales.

Of course the nature of criminality and the nature of people's contact with and perception of the criminal justice system changed. Vagrancy, an old offence, was still a major problem in the early part of the twentieth century but had become, as a result of changes in the method of dealing with poverty rather than its elimination, the material for nostalgic reminiscence about colourful local tramps by the end.[10] On the other hand, the growth of the volume and the regulation of motor vehicles brought more and more people, many of whom would not have considered themselves "criminal" in some sort of Victorian positivism typology, into the criminal courts.[11] The prosecution of motoring offences was becoming noticeable across Wales. Radnorshire police were empowered to purchase four stopwatches to conduct speed checks in 1903. P.C. Hall of Drefach was using the speedometer of his motor cycle to convict motorists around Newcastle Emlyn in 1929, whilst plain-clothes speed traps were employed in Merionethshire in 1941, and some 2,000 parking violations occurred in the year following the new parking regulations introduced into Swansea town centre in 1965.[12] It is easy to overlook the significance of such material, but in its regularization of the penetration of the criminal law into the normality of everyday life it demands our attention. In the same vein, the mobility of the police force itself extended its operational reach, and its communication with other forces, considerably. The police bicycle was hailed as "an inestimable boon" by the Chief Constable of Cardiganshire in his report in 1900, and ten new "Swifts" were purchased by the Caernarfonshire force in the same year. These machines were added to by the motorcycles and cars of later decades; Cardiff had established a mobile police squad in 1932, Merionethshire became the last force in Wales to acquire a car in 1939.[13] Other work of the police brought them into more routine contact with the populace, even in rural areas. Responsibilities in respect of animals, including dogs, were important here. In 1908 Merioneth police supervised the dipping of 765,937 sheep, whilst rural police might keep records of sheep earmarks, as at Talybont in Cardiganshire. Radnorshire police had to be issued with haversacks to carry the forms associated with dipping.[14]

None of this, of course, is to suggest that familiarity with the police invariably promoted harmony. Early in the century constables were hired to protect their interests by industrialists in both North and South Wales, a

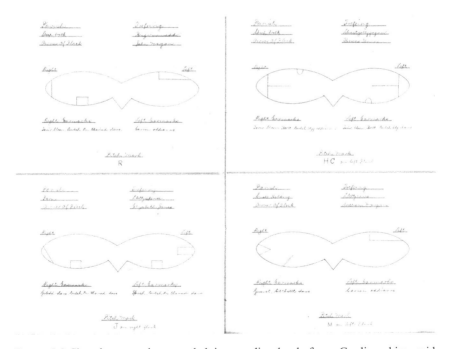

Figure 5.1 Sheep's earmarks recorded in a police book from Cardiganshire, mid-twentieth century. The proforma is in English, the annotation in Welsh.
Courtesy Ceredigion Archives and Dyfed Powys Police.

practice which was hardly designed to promote confidence in their impartiality when policing industrial disputes more generally.[15] Such disputes produced some notable public order clashes from early on in the century, continuing a practice which has been noted in the previous chapter. A protracted and bitter struggle featuring quarrymen in Bethesda from 1901–1903 necessitated a call for assistance from outside the local force, including, interestingly, Welsh-speaking officers from Liverpool.[16] Outside assistance, from the Metropolitan Police and, in a move which was to prove controversial for the reputation of the then Home Secretary Winston Churchill for decades, the army, was also called upon in the events known as the Tonypandy Riots. A series of actions precipitated by an industrial dispute with the Cambrian Combine collieries in 1910 saw its most serious rioting and the death of a miner on 8 November 1910, although the strike, the disturbances and the trials, which *inter alia* saw two of the miners' leaders imprisoned, went on well into 1911.[17] In August 1911 riots flared, too, in Llanelli following a national rail strike and intensi-fied after the shooting dead of two men. Other fatalities followed when arson caused an explosion. The local press were again keen to blame the violence on outsiders and the *Llanelly Star* criticized the fact that the county police were based in Llandeilo, "with a population of about three men and a dog", a comment which confirms the perception of a division between industrial and rural Wales and the failure of the authorities properly to respond to the changes caused by the growth of the former. On the same day as Llanelli erupted, anti-Jewish riots were beginning in Tredegar. Such a conjunction is indi-cative both of a strong sense of "community" solidarity and a reminder of some of the limitations on the sense of inclusivity of the notion of community.[18]

This last example reminds us that, whilst many of the public order dis-turbances witnessed within this period were connected with industrial disputes (in a work of this nature the responsibility for such disturbances and the question of whether the criminal justice system and its servants were appro-priately deployed in each case cannot be adequately investigated), not all riots fall within this pattern. In an extraordinary incident in March 1919 Canadian soldiers, eager to be returned home after demobilization from the Great War and in possession of ammunition which been sent to their camp at Kinmel Park in North Wales, ironically as a precaution against industrial disorder, were involved in a mutiny. Five of their number were admitted to have been killed, 21 wounded and 51 subsequently court-martialled as the uprising was suppressed. Interestingly, not only were red flags flown during the insurrec-tion, but some of the participants wore women's clothing.[19] Such displays of ritual behaviour, perhaps unexpected in the Canadian forces, were still, in a tradition we have seen throughout the nineteenth century, to be found in Welsh popular protests of the twentieth. A picture of the Tonypandy picket of 7 November 1910 appears to show two strikers with blackened faces and wearing shrouds in the mass of people outside the Glamorgan colliery. In a similar vein, "whiteshirting", the parading of a scrupulously cleanly attired "blackleg" in a wheelbarrow before striking communities, as well as

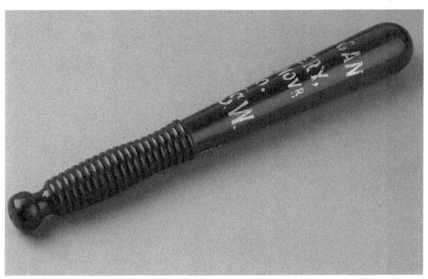

Figure 5.2 Black (and blue) humour? The presentation of a miniature truncheon by Chief Constable Lionel Lindsay to one "S.W." after the Tonypandy riots of 1910 in which a miner died might be considered to be in dubious taste. Courtesy South Wales Police Museum.

boycotting and ostracism were features of some of these twentieth-century industrial encounters, in which procedures the role of women was a notable component. Hywel Francis reported the resilience of these traditions in the miners' strike of 1984–1985, and cites an occasion when a *cymanfa ganu*, a traditional choral assembly, took place outside a strikebreaker's house in order to evade restrictions on public assembly. On occasion the tradition of local dissent was more expressly invoked. In 1926 strikers in Ammanford were using the name of "Scotch Cattle", whilst in 1935 disturbances at Blaina (Monmouthshire) around the new Unemployment Act, which saw 11 men imprisoned, saw the invocation of the spirit of Chartism of a century earlier. In the rural context, the tradition of Rebecca was echoed by poachers, operating in disguise but apparently happy to be seen and photographed publicly, in twentieth-century Radnorshire[20] It may be noted in parenthesis that, if radicalism could apparently descend through generations – that it was in a sense in the Welsh blood – then at least one voice in the '30s was calling for a eugenic solution to the overproduction of the children of the "unfit" classes, which expressly included Welsh miners. "Fitness" here seems to bear a moral rather than a physical weight.[21]

It was perhaps not too difficult to keep alive traditions of opposition when that opposition was so regularly evidenced. In the disputes over coal the law frequently played a crucial part, both in its operation and evasion. There was an attempt to invoke the provisions of the Munitions of War Act to outlaw a strike in the

Figure 5.3 Disguised poachers pose for the camera, Radnorshire, twentieth century. Courtesy The Judge's Lodging, Presteigne.

South Wales coalfield in 1915. Ten years later another strike saw violence in the anthracite areas of Ammanford and Glynneath, and the Deputy Chief Constable of Carmarthenshire was severely beaten. The events of 1926 saw considerable violence as Welsh miners continued the dispute which had led to the General Strike. Police were brought in from outside the area and the Chief Constable of Glamorgan, who with his counterparts in Carmarthenshire and Monmouthshire earned a reputation for particular hostility to the strikers, instituted surveillance of "seditious" persons whom he believed to be behind the stoppage. As well as the physical injury caused by the violence, which included a murder, and the polarization of the attitudes between mining communities and the police which would adversely affect the wider interaction between the two, the 1926 strike and lockout saw a rise in the "subsistence" offence of poaching and even sheep-stealing. In sentencing Elmira Bailey to two months' imprisonment in Treorchy, the judge commented: "I find that the women have been taking too prominent part in these disturbances and I must impose a penalty that will be a deterrent to others"[22] The bitter miners' strike of 1984–1985 witnessed great displays of communal solidarity in which again women played a notable part, but it too saw violence: the killing of a taxi-driver, whose vehicle was carrying a working miner, by a block dropped from a motorway overbridge, resulted in the creation of an important precedent in the law of homicide. Antipathy towards strikebreakers continued even after the return to work, and it is reported that most of those in South Wales eventually moved away.[23]

In this and others of the larger industrial disturbances the local police force were assisted by officers drafted in from other forces. This also happened at the investiture of the Prince of Wales in 1911 and again in 1969, though, in relation to the latter instance, as we shall see, concern over surrounding militancy and the failure of Welsh forces to make a breakthrough had seen the setting up of a Special Unit based over the border in Shrewsbury. The intervention of outside forces in more routine cases was less frequent but not unknown. Two cases in the 1920s had involved the Metropolitan Police being directed by the Home Office, in a departure from the normal procedure of intervention by invitation only. One of these was the Greenwood poisoning case from Carmarthenshire in 1920, when the accused, in another instance which caused discussion of the operation of the Welsh jury, was acquitted. A brief but remarkable surviving film of the accused's arrival in court, with the rather chaotic display by the official trumpeters, hardly promotes the image of a modern legal system. Neither did the, apparently unsuccessful, local petition of more than 3,000 in Monmouthshire to bring in the Metropolitan Police to investigate another case in 1926.[24] The question of the reputation of Welsh policing and justice clearly deserves to be considered.

The small size of many of the Welsh forces had been a source of unease for some time before action was taken to address it, discussion of amalgamation going back as far as the 1920s. Montgomeryshire, Breconshire and Radnorshire were formed into the Mid-Wales Constabulary in 1948, whilst in the north, Anglesey, Caernarfonshire and Merionethshire formed the Gwynedd Constabulary in 1950, which also incorporated Flintshire and Denbighshire in 1967, becoming North Wales Police in 1974, a process which provided a neat geographical counterpoint to South Wales Police, which had been formed after reconfiguration in 1969. Gwent Police was the name ultimately given to the amalgamation of the Monmouthshire and Newport Borough forces, which had originally taken place in 1967. The most interesting events, however, took place in Cardiganshire, which, with a grand total of 75 officers, two of them women, in 1957, was the smallest in England and Wales. Two inquiries were held in that year into the operation of the force after a dispute over the appointment of a Deputy Chief Constable escalated into allegations of misconduct and laxity on the part of the Chief Constable and revealed details, *inter alia*, of members of the motor patrol being "accommodated overnight at the Glyndwr Hotel, Machynlleth, in the company of two women". Having heard that there was a "serious loss of public confidence" in the force, the Home Office moved to amalgamate it with the neighbouring Carmarthenshire Constabulary, despite the opposition of the two counties.[25] The merger followed in 1958, and in 1968 the Mid-Wales and Pembrokeshire forces were also added, to form the geographically largest police area in England and Wales, which changed its name to Dyfed-Powys Police in 1974.[26]

If the police were on occasion open to criticism, so too were the magistracy. It is true that some very distinguished individuals sat on Welsh benches at times; the great common law judge Lord Atkin is best remembered for cases of more constitutional significance than when, sitting with his colleagues on the Tywyn bench near his family home in 1935, he fined "Countess Barcynska"

£2 for illegally posting playbills, yet he did.[27] More generally, however, the established Welsh attitude of regarding a criminal prosecution as being part of a process of negotiation rather than the culmination of a formal process seems to have continued into the twentieth century. An anonymous author claimed in 1932 that:

> the practice of approaching local J.P.s before the case comes on at petty sessions on the part of complainants or defendants does prevail ... The thing is becoming notorious, and unless unchecked will bring the administration of justice in law courts into universal contempt.[28]

The Duparq Commission some 15 years later reported a similar finding, at least outside Glamorgan, which led Lord Exeter to declare it to be "a very great scandal and brings the administration of justice into disrepute". In 1946 uproar followed the dismissal of a case by the Justices of Aberaeron (Cardiganshire). The case had involved the slaughter of a pig contrary to food regulations then in place and the defendant held the offices of both Food Executive Officer and the Clerk to the Justices. The newly appointed Lord Chief Justice, Lord Goddard, on the case being stated for review by a superior court, spoke of "a state of affairs which appears to me to be as shocking as I have come across for a very long time". Subsequently a public inquiry under Lord Justice Tucker was set up to investigate the proceedings, which largely exonerated the bench, at least of any grave malpractice.[29] It is interesting to note in passing that Elwyn Jones, later Lord Chancellor, who appeared before the inquiry, wrote later that he had found little to complain about in the behaviour of Welsh juries who took their duties "seriously and responsibly", despite Roderick Bowen's entertaining animadversions on the subject mentioned earlier. He did concede, however, that there could be linguistic difficulties (on occasion not without humour) in Welsh-speaking areas.[30]

The controversy surrounding the impartiality of the Welsh magistracy did not end there. *The Times* reported in 1970 that, after the imprisonment of the popular singer Dafydd Iwan for refusal to pay a £56 fine for defacing a road sign as part of the language activism to be discussed below, no fewer than 21 magistrates had contributed to a fund set up to pay that fine.[31] Yet, as in earlier periods, the magistrates' own use of the Welsh language could assist in the operation of the administration of justice in cases which they tried. The long-running question of the use of the language in legal proceedings was not going to disappear. Agnes Crompton, convicted of theft of an easy chair from Borth (Cardiganshire) railway station, appealed in 1918 on the grounds that not all of the jury could understand English. I have failed to discover the outcome of the case, but a conviction was quashed on similar grounds in a subsequent case from 1933. This latter decision drew the adverse comment of Sir Thomas Artemus Jones, who had himself, on becoming a judge in North Wales, declared that he would, contrary to statute, allow Welsh to be used in court and did so. He was not alone, for Caernarfonshire Quarter Sessions, under the Chairmanship of Lloyd George, had decided so to proceed in a case from 1933, being thwarted only by the absence of a Welsh-speaking shorthand writer. The formal prohibition on the use of Welsh in the courts was relaxed by the Welsh Language Act of 1942, although only to the extent, rather narrowly interpreted by the higher judiciary, that a party or witness might otherwise suffer a disadvantage. This condition was removed by the Act of 1967, although under that statute prior notice had to be given of the desire to use Welsh before superior courts. The 1967 Welsh Language Act itself however did not satisfy critics, and the deputy clerk of the peace for Pembrokeshire advised in an article in the *New Law Journal* that experience of Assize cases had shown that in practice a defendant would be well advised not to exercise his right to use Welsh.[32] The right to use Welsh in court proceedings was confirmed in the Welsh Language Act 1993.

As the Dafydd Iwan case reminds us, however, the status of the Welsh language was an issue not only for the conduct of proceedings within the courts but also one which brought individuals, often those who did not consider themselves as "criminal" in any essentialist sense, before the court in the first place. Campaigns of civil disobedience in defence of the language became familiar from the 1960s, from the celebrated protest by *Cymdeithas yr Iaith Cymraeg* (The Welsh Language Society) which blocked Trefechan bridge in Aberystwyth in February 1963 to the defacing of English-language roadsigns (over 100 were targeted in Cardiganshire in one week in 1969), a refusal to tax motor vehicles using monolingual forms and to purchase the television licence fee as agitation grew for improved Welsh-language broadcasting. Often, as originally with Iwan's case, fines were unpaid and by 1976 some 697 people had appeared in court and 143 were imprisoned for their part in the society's protests.[33] A total of 51 were imprisoned for contempt after singing in court at the appearance as defendants of Dafydd Iwan and seven other members of the society in the case at Carmarthen in April 1972. Subsequently the trial was transferred to Swansea, although the judge who sanctioned that jurisdictional move accepted that a Welsh-speaking judge would preside at the resulting proceedings.[34]

Cymdeithas yr Iaith had rejected the use of violence in 1966, but for some individuals and groups complex and shifting admixtures of language and cultural concerns, nationalism and republicanism, might produce more alarming instances of illegality than those discussed above. One of the seminal events of twentieth-century Welsh protest, though it involved no interpersonal violence, was the arson attack on the bombing school being built on the Lleyn peninsula in North Wales in 1936, symbolically 400 years after the first Henrician Act of Union. Three high-profile individuals, Saunders Lewis, D.J. Williams and the Rev. Lewis Valentine, surrendered themselves to the police as perpetrators of the arson. The judge at the subsequent trial in Caernarfon, though he refused to accept the pleas of the defendants in Welsh, did accept that the jury should speak the language. After an emotional trial, in which Lewis addressed them directly and specifically, the jury failed to agree on a verdict. The case was removed to London for retrial "in the interests of justice", although the Lord Chief Justice declined to expand further upon his reasons for making that ruling. The defendants were convicted and sentenced to nine months' imprisonment.[35]

An event of similar cultural relevance came with the decision in 1957, against strong local opposition, to create a reservoir for Liverpool's water supply by flooding the Tryweryn valley in Merionethshire. Damage was done on the site in late 1962 and in February of 1963 a bomb blew up a transformer, an attack which was followed by a further attempt to destroy a pylon the next month. Three men from the *Mudiad Amddyffin Cymru* (MAC, Movement for the Defence of Wales) were imprisoned in consequence of the activities. In the years that followed a number of shadowy organizations (and some not so shadowy: the "Free Wales Army", which appeared in uniform at the opening of the Treweryn reservoir in 1965, assiduously courted publicity), of uncertain membership, connection and wider affiliation, were responsible for a variety of actions. There was a threat to poison the proposed Clywedog reservoir in Montgomeryshire by *Meibion Glyndwr* (MG, The Sons of Glyndwr) also in 1962, and 4 years later a bomb exploded at that site. Water had become one of the major focuses of protests, seen as a Welsh natural resource being appropriated by the English at a social and cultural cost, and pipes were attacked again in September 1967.[36]

There was an increase in the frequency and range of militant activity in the run up to the Investiture of Prince Charles as Prince of Wales at Caernarfon in 1969. Bombs exploded in Cardiff at targets which included the Welsh Office and the city's Police Headquarters, and a serviceman was injured by a device which went off at RAF Pembrey (Carmarthenshire). Concern about the efficacy of the Welsh police response was voiced, and a Special Unit set up outside Wales to co-ordinate the efforts against the bombers. The extent of the activities of this Shrewsbury unit were to cause some unease within Wales; a powerful poster warned of its operations under the heading, "If You're Welsh You're Watched".[37]

On the day before the Investiture, 30 June 1969, two men, George Taylor and Alwyn Jones, were killed in Abergele (Denbighshire) when explosives they were carrying near the railway line to be used by the royal train detonated. In April 1970 John Jenkins, the Anglophone director of operations of the MAC, was sentenced to 10 years' imprisonment and another man to 6 years' for offences connected with the bombing campaign.[38]

The next phase of militancy came in a programme of instances of arson, largely directed against holiday homes in the period between 1979 and 1992. In 1988 the attacks were extended to target estate agents in England, both on the borders and in London. In total some 197 instances were recorded within this period. Although the campaign was largely associated with MG, there were other organizations, *Cadwyr Cymru* and the "Workers Army of the Welsh Republic", whose names were connected with some activities, not all of which shared the same aim or target. It was difficult to penetrate the cells

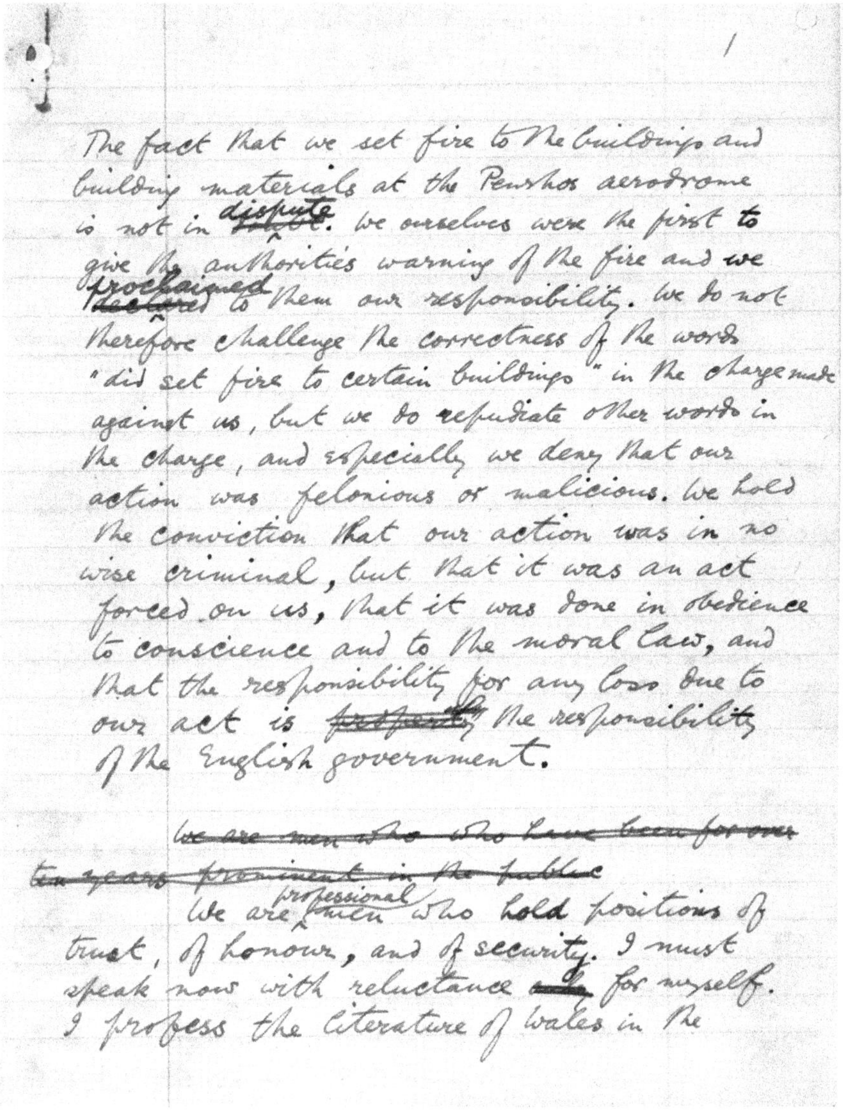

The fact that we set fire to the buildings and building materials at the Penrhos aerodrome is not in ~~dispute~~ dispute. We ourselves were the first to give the authorities warning of the fire and we ~~declared~~ proclaimed to them our responsibility. We do not therefore challenge the correctness of the words "did set fire to certain buildings" in the charge made against us, but we do repudiate other words in the charge, and especially we deny that our action was felonious or malicious. We hold the conviction that our action was in no wise criminal, but that it was an act forced on us, that it was done in obedience to conscience and to the moral law, and that the responsibility for any loss due to our act is ~~felt fully~~ the responsibility of the English government.

~~We are men who who have been for ten years prominent in the public~~
We are professional ~~men~~ who hold positions of trust, of honour, and of security. I must speak now with reluctance ~~only~~ for myself. I profess the literature of Wales in the

Figure 5.4 The draft of the speech made to the court at Caernarfon in 1936 by Saunders Lewis following the arson at the bombing school.
Courtesy the Estate of Saunders Lewis. Image supplied by Llyfrgell Genedlaethol Cymru/National Library of Wales.

responsible for carrying out attacks, and Roy Davies, head of Llanelli CID at the time, admitted that "There was absolutely no co-operation by the public when crimes such as the burning of holiday homes was committed". The police responded with "Operation Tân" in 1980, a massive swoop on known nationalists, but despite such an action only one person, Sion Roberts, was ever convicted of offences connected with the arson campaign, and that as late as 1993.[39]

Major police operations were also to take place in relation to a very different variety of crime which was also becoming more noticeable in the second half of the century. Drugs offences had, as a report of 1973 pointed out, once largely been associated with the port areas of Cardiff and Swansea, but as time went on it became, in Wales as elsewhere, less geographically and socially circumscribed.[40] Detective Chief Supt Pat Molloy, in charge of Dyfed-Powys CID, had no problems in allocating the blame: "We had our drugs problems. We had more than our fair share of social drop-outs and the dross of an overloaded and costly higher education system". A female student in the late 1960s saw it rather differently: "What else is there to do in Aberystwyth in the middle of winter but men and drink and the odd little puff of grass?"[41] A Drug Squad was set up in Cardiff in 1967 and in North Wales in 1971, although in 1974 only 578 persons were found guilty of drugs offences in Welsh Courts. Detective Inspector Humphreys in 1988 linked the Deeside drugs problems to Liverpool and Manchester, and that in Holyhead to Dublin.[42] Although we have noted the tendency to blame "outsiders" for Welsh criminality, there seems to be some support, at least on an anecdotal level, from law enforcement officials for the idea that demographic changes, which saw the country being viewed as a focus for an "alternative" counterculture may have contributed to the spread of this variety of offending. One rural Probation Officer, interviewed towards the end of the century, spoke of clients in his area:

> The inhabitants of these isolated properties tend to be incomers, rather than locals, many of whom are involved in the drug scene and, frequently, its associated violence ... in some instances it is not the clients themselves but their "business associates" and dealers who may present the greatest possible danger.[43]

Undoubtedly many of the narcotics themselves came into Wales from outside. It was rumoured that drugs distributed through Swansea, "the drugs capital of South Wales", came in through the means of small boats operating on the Welsh coast, and in 1983 the discovery of equipment and a man-made cave at Seal Bay in Pembrokeshire made such a belief credible and led to a major investigation. It is clear, though, that drugs could be exported from Wales as well as imported. "Operation Julie" involved 11 police forces in the pursuit of a massive LSD manufacturing operation based near Tregaron (Cardiganshire). The raids on premises in March 1977 and the substantial prison sentences which followed marked the conclusion of a complex undercover police inquiry into offenders, some at least of whom claimed to have been driven by ideological rather than financial motives. Three other significant drugs rings were broken by South Wales Police in 1981.[44]

Such spectacular events should not, of course, distract us from the banal familiarity of much of twentieth-century crime in Wales, the petty thefts and assaults which for centuries, as we have seen, present themselves like the common cold of social pathology. The uncomfortable truth was that, even in times of national emergency, crime continued, not only in black-marketeering but also, in Swansea, in burglary within the blackout and the looting of bombed premises, even from a mined ship, and theft of materials for local defence. The Chief Constable of Caernarfonshire in 1940 blamed the occurrence of juvenile crime on evacuees, many of whom had been removed to Wales from English cities.[45]

It is tempting to think, in the way that commentators such as Henry Richard had urged in the nineteenth century, that there was an immense gulf in criminality between urban and rural areas of Wales. Quantitavely there is support for the idea of crime as a phenomenon of the cities, or, as we have noted, the associated housing estates serving them. But a survey in Aberystwyth in 1993 by Laurence Koffman, using a victim survey rather than official figures of reported crime, revealed that, by and large, the *nature* of crime experienced in this semi-rural area was similar to that revealed by similar surveys in England and Wales as a whole. The majority of offences reported were against property, particularly motor vehicles, with only 10 per cent of reported incidents being instances of violence, though one third of these involved no significant injury. Only 45 per cent of the instances revealed by the survey had been reported to the police. More encouragingly, the survey found less fear of crime, becoming regarded as a social problem in itself independent of actual victimization, than in urban areas of Wales, although such fear was not consistently distributed across age and sex of respondents.[46] If such an analysis serves again to counsel us to distrust the myth of "*Cymru Lân*", "Pure Wales", there are still occasions when we catch glimpses, as we have when looking at shaming practices, of an old Wales even in the twentieth century, though again they are not presented as in any sense typical here. In 1948 one Geraldine Worrall, described as "a gypsy" was sentenced to nine months' imprisonment at Pembrokeshire Assizes for obtaining more than £1,800 from a spinster to whom she had held out the promise of a "husband and a large fortune" The judge declared the case reminiscent of "the Dark Ages of medieval times". Almost a decade later a man failed to appear in court in North Wales as he was consulting a "cunning woman" about his health.[47]

Of course there were instances of very serious crimes throughout the century, and some of these certainly occurred in rural districts. It is not my intention to take the reader through a catalogue of grisly and bizarre homicides which have been committed in Wales: prurience and sensationalism too easily take the place of analysis in histories of crime. But there are cases which are suggestive of attitudes which are worth pausing over. One of these is the degree of communal involvement which might attend a murder investigation. This could, perhaps, be no more than a reflection of such prurience and sensationalism in others, in the same way that the jeering crowd, which still greets the prison van (almost invariably with one person breaking through to bang on its side) when an offender leaves court, can be regarded in the same light. But such social events may have deeper social meaning and historical resonance. A degree of community participation in the processes of criminal justice has been argued to be a striking element of Carmarthenshire life in the nineteenth century.[48] In a murder case from the same county in 1953, Thomas Ronald Harries of Pendine (Carms) was convicted after the murder of a farmer and his wife, whose bodies had been buried in a field. "Hundreds of farmers and other helpers" were involved in the extensive search for the victims, a search carefully recorded in a series of police photographic slides, and some 4,000 people were reported to have watched Harries leave the court having been sentenced to death.[49] He was hanged at Swansea in 1954, the penultimate person to meet that fate in Wales. The last, 24-year-old Vivian Teed, who had been convicted of the brutal murder of a sub-postmaster, died at Swansea in May 1958.[50]

One other murder merits discussion (and also, incidentally, invites reflection on the historical morality of liability to the death sentence). In 1988 Lynette White, working as a prostitute in Cardiff, was murdered and five men were charged with the murder, three of whom were convicted in 1990, but released on appeal in 1992. Subsequently a massive investigation into alleged police malpractice in the case identified 121 serving or retired officers as persons of interest, but the prosecution of the 13 charged was discontinued after the collapse of the trial of the first eight in December 2011 on the grounds that evidence had not been disclosed to the defence and could not be found. An Independent Police Complaints Commission, published as this book was going to press, found that the collapse of the trial was not attributable to deliberate wrongdoing, though mistakes had been made.[51]

Apart from in respect of the death penalty, there were other changes taking place within the penal system. Before discussing imprisonment in general it may be interesting to mention some particular establishments which fell outside the normal range of institutions. Frongoch, near Bala (Merionethshire), on a site which had once housed the Royal Welsh Whisky factory, had served as a former German Prisoner of War (POW) Camp. In June 1916 it took custody of Irish Republicans, to number 1,863 in all, detained after the Easter Rising and held under the Defence of the Realm Act. The choice of location for such a camp in a Welsh-speaking heartland seems strange, although the Welsh as a whole seem to have been largely against the Irish insurrection. Aware of their surroundings, the internees added Welsh lessons to the cultural and military ethos within the camp, from which they were released at Christmas of that year. Later Irish internees were held at institutions including Usk, from which four escaped, in breach of the parole they had given to the authorities, in January 1919.[52] There were several POW camps for enemy personnel in Wales in the Second World War, the most famous perhaps being Island Farm Camp, Bridgend, from which around 70 detainees escaped in March 1945.[53] Famous for a rather different reason is the POW camp at Henllan (Cards), where the Italian prisoners constructed a remarkable decorated chapel, which still survives, from waste materials.

As to the more regular provision of prison premises, the process of closure of local gaols which had begun in the nineteenth century continued into the twentieth. Brecon and Ruthin both closed in 1916. Carmarthen, Caernarfon and Usk all closed in 1922, all traces of John Nash's work at the first-mentioned being lost. But Usk reopened in 1939 as a closed borstal and subsequently became a Detention Centre, Youth Custody Centre and Young Offender Institution, and then again as an adult prison, latterly in association with the nearby former open borstal. Concern about juvenile offenders had, as we have seen, been developing from the previous century. Some juveniles had in the late-nineteenth and early twentieth centuries been sent to work on Welsh farms from English Industrial Schools, no doubt as a perceived "healthy" extraction from their normal environments and influences.[54] Provision of more traditional penal establishments for local juvenile offenders in the populous south of Wales remained generally poor, however, being noted to be so in the 1930s and '40s. Attendance centres in Swansea and Cardiff, the population of the adult prisons of which two places had doubled between 1946 and 1962, were taking a total of only 100 boys per year in the 1950s.[55]

The consolidation of adult prison provision due to a "rationalization" of the national service saw custodial provision in Wales limited to the south of the country only, in Cardiff and Swansea. This meant that prisoners from other areas were often committed to remands or sentences in English prisons, such as Shrewsbury, which left prisoners' families often making long journeys to visit detainees, who themselves in some circumstances might experience linguistic difficulties in English institutions. Provision for women prisoners from Wales was particularly affected. HMP Parc, the only prison to date built in Wales under the Private Finance Initiative, was opened near Bridgend in November 1997, bringing back into the country an ideology of penal economy which had disappeared after the time of John Howard.

The problems of providing a uniform, cost-efficient, centralized service within a country the topography and demography of which was not conducive to the task affected non-custodial as well as custodial sentence provision. A study of the operation of the probation service in a rural Welsh area towards the end of the century revealed problems caused by the distances between clients, officers and resources such as bail hostels. One officer described the skills needed to visit some clients as a combination of "orienteering, rallying and animal taming". Interestingly, there was also the suggestion that local "celebrities" of a kind who would not be notable in an urban setting might expect strings to be pulled in administration of an order so as to minimise embarrassment or inconvenience. There remains the hint of the survival of a principle which we have noted before, which sees the legal process as a basis of negotiation rather than a statement of authority.

More seriously, Welsh local government itself has not always escaped criticism. In 1974 a request was made to the Home Secretary to set up a standing commission into corruption in Wales, and an allegation in the House of Commons 20 years later that there was a "tradition of corruption and sleaze" in some South Wales local councils led to a walk-out of opposition MPs from the chamber. In 1975 six councillors from South Wales were charged along with ten others of offences including conspiracy, corruption and deception, and in 1977 there was a prosecution of 22 former councillors, officials and company directors for corruption and related offences.[56] "Looking after one's own" is not a universally laudable phenomenon.

There is a great deal that this chapter has not addressed. Jokes are sometimes to be heard about canny farmers exploiting bureaucratic naivety over agricultural subsidies, or agricultural "red" diesel being used improperly, but I have no idea how much, if any, truth supports them. On the other hand, there are accounts of fuel oil and other products, including livestock, being easy pickings for thieves who target farms and other properties in rural and remote locations. There are encouraging signs that rural and farm crime are beginning to attract the attention of contemporary criminologists, but it is a subject concerning which future historians may have rather more detailed information upon which to base their opinions than is currently available. Detailed research which may reveal the reality behind the anecdote is necessary, for we should remember that not all claims relating to the incidence and nature of criminality survive the judgement of history. The *Evening Express* claimed in 1927, for example, that Cardiff was the centre of the "white slave traffic", but the idea would seem never to have been substantiated.[57]

However, recent developments counsel that our knowledge may sometimes be only partial, even when it might seem to belong to events located in the past. Recognition of that uncomfortable fact haunts the legal historian even as it consoles him or her. Many of the events discussed in this and earlier chapters have been spoken of as closed: new sources may be discovered, existing ones reinterpreted or their accuracy questioned, but in the majority of cases we know pretty much all we can do about the events of the distant past. "Facts" are the product of points in time. Yet those who, like myself, feel more comfortable writing about criminality of earlier times than in its present or recent manifestations should remember that an "official" version of the past may still remain contingent. As I write, investigations are taking place into allegations of sexual abuse in children's homes in North Wales dating back as far as the 1960s and into the earlier responses to those allegations. Some of these matters were the subject of one report which was suppressed for many years before being released in 2013 in a redacted form, and of another later investigation which resulted in the publication of *Lost in Care: The Waterhouse Report* in February 2000. There may be more to be revealed in the future about the events of the past.[58]

Notes

1 D.J.V. Jones, *Crime and Policing in the Twentieth Century*, p. 287. See Jones's careful statistical analyses, both in this volume and in "Where did it all go wrong? Crime in Swansea 1938–68" *Welsh History Review* (1990) 15: 240. See also the discussions in M. Johnes, *Wales Since 1939* (Manchester: Manchester University Press, 2012) esp. pp. 99, 363.

2 For an overall view, see, e.g., Davies, *History*, Chs 9 and 10. It is difficult to improve on Jones's comment on the response to the rise: "In truth, the roots of criminal behaviour in an increasingly prosperous welfare state are defyingly complex. In the circumstances, it was easier to rely on the centuries-old view that crime was an activity closely related to the changing moral climate", Jones, "Where did it all go wrong?" p. 266.

3 *Police Cadet* (BBC, broadcast 9 January 1967) NSSAW V_/DIG/A/14703.

4 See Ireland, "Putting oneself on whose country" p. 70, n. 21.

5 Jones, *Crime and Policing*, pp. 117–119, Johnes, *Wales Since 1939*, pp. 371–372.

6 Jones, "Where did it all go wrong?" p. 248 on burglary in Swansea in the 1960s; gangs from Lancashire and the Midlands were supposed to be present in Abersoch and Rhyl in 1969; Birch, *History of Policing*, p. 317. For the A55, see D. Hughes, "The effect of infrastructure development on crime in rural areas: A case study of the A55 Coastal Expressway in North Wales" *Cambrian Law Review* (1996) 27: 33 at pp. 53–54.

7 *Cambrian News*, 28 April 1905. Cf. the account in R. Davies, "'In a broken dream': Some aspects of sexual behaviour and the dilemmas of the unmarried mother in South West Wales, 1887–1914" *Llafur* (1983) 3: 24 at p. 25.

8 A.D. Rees, *Life in a Welsh Countryside* (Cardiff: University of Wales Press, 1961) p. 83.

9 I. Emmet, *A North Wales Village: A Social Anthropological Study* (London: Routledge 1964) p. 89. For poaching, see Ch. 5.

10 Jones, *Crime and Policing*, p. 168; compare for example M. Muller, "A few gentlemen of the road" *Pembrokeshire Life*, April 2006, p. 14.

11 The great footballer Ivor Allchurch was prosecuted for a driving offence in 1954! See Jones, "Where did it all go wrong?" p. 255.

12 Maddox, *A History of the Radnorshire Constabulary* (Llandrindod Wells: Radnorshire Society, 1959) p. 50, K. Jones, *Newcastle Emlyn*, pp. 273–274, Birch, *History of Policing*, p. 194–195, Jones, "Where did it all go wrong?" p. 255.

13 *Chief Constables Report*, p. 18, Birch, *History of Policing*, p .182, 265–266, Jones, *Crime and Policing*, p. 29.

14 Birch, *History of Policing*, p. 179, Ceredigion Archives POL/9/4 and also, for records of dipping and animal movement, Maddox, *A History of the Radnorshire Constabulary*, p. 57.

15 Ibid., p. 180, Jones, *Crime and Policing*, p. 190.

16 Birch, *History of Policing*, p. 220.

17 G. Evans and D. Maddox, *The Tonypandy Riots 1910–1911* (Plymouth: University of Plymouth Press, 2010).

18 D. Hopkin, "The Llanelli Riots 1911" *Welsh History Review* (1983) 11: 488 at p. 501, W. Rubenstein, "The anti-Jewish riots of 1911 in South Wales: a re-examination" *Welsh History Review* (1997) 18: 667, which argues for an economic rather than an entrenched anti-semitic motive. Thre had been anti-Jewish violence in Dowlais in 1903, and would be racially motivated violence in Cardiff and Barry in 1919 (see Jones, *Crime and Policing*, pp. 130–131). The Chief Constable of Cardiff, praising the operation of the Special Restriction (Coloured Alien Seamen) Order 1925 expressed concern about the "mingling of the white and coloured races in the Shipping Quarter" in 1928 (Jones, *Crime and Policing*, p. 230). See also, more generally, U. Henriques "The Jews and crime in South Wales before World War I" *Morgannwg* (1985) xxix: 59.

19 J. Putkowski, *The Kinmel Park Riots 1919* (Hawarden: Flintshire Historical Society, 1998) and note p. 26.

20 Evans and Maddox, *Tonypandy Riots*, p. 59; Jones, "Women, community and collective action" pp. 35–36; S. Bruley, *The Women and Men of 1926: A Gender and Social History of the General Strike and Miners' Lockout in South Wales* (Cardiff: University of Wales Press, 2010) pp. 109–110; H. Francis, "The law, oral tradition and the mining community" *Journal of Law and Society* (1985) 12: 267; Davies, *Wales*, p. 555; D. Preece, "Defend the rights of the roads your fathers fought for": The Blaina riot of 1935" *Llafur* (2010) 73; Maddox, *A History of the Radnorshire Constabulary*, plates 5 and 6.

21 G. Williams, "Compulsory sterilisation of Welsh miners, 1936" *Llafur* (1982): 67. The idea recalls the "anthropological" discussion of the previous century, see "F.P.C." "The Celt of Ireland and the Celt of Wales" *Covnhill Magazine* (1877): 674.

22 Bruley, *Women and Men*, p. 77, 108; Davies, *Wales*, pp. 516–517, 550–557; Jones, *Crime and Policing*, p. 66; J. McIlroy, A. Campbell and K. Gildart, *Industrial Politics and the 1926 Mining Lockout: The Struggle for Dignity* (Cardiff: University of Wales Press, 2009) Chs 5, 6, 11.

23 *R. v Hancock and Shankland* [1986] 1 A.C. 455; Johnes, *Wales Since 1939*, pp. 260–267; Davies, *Wales*, pp. 683–685.

24 G. Rubin, "Calling in the Met: serious crime involving Scotland Yard and provincial police forces in England and Wales, 1906–1939" *Legal Studies* (2011) 31: 411. For the film, see NSSAW V__/16_/A/6302. For a more usual instance of the Met. being invited to assist, see the O'Brien murder of 1946; Maddox, *History of Radnorshire Constabulary*, p. 72.

25 Birch, *History of Policing*, pp. 261–262, Ch. X; Jones, *Crime and Policing*, Preface. C. Griffiths, *Heddluoedd Canolbarth a Gorllewin Cymru 1829–1974/The Police Forces of Mid and West Wales* (Llandybie: Dinefwr Publishers, 2008). For the Cardiganshire Dispute, see *The Times*, 23 August, 17, 18 December 1957.

26 For the wider context of police reorganization, see P. Rawlings, *Policing: A Short History* (Cullompton: Willan, 2002) Chs 6 and 7.

27 J. Harris, "'A venture of love and youth and spring: Countess Barcynska's repertory players, 1935–6" *Ceredigion* (2012) xvi: 133 at p. 141–142.

28 "Demos" "The Welsh magistracy" *The Welsh Outlook* (1932) xix: 204 at p.205.

29 R. Jones, "The strange case of a wartime pig and a judicial inquiry into the conduct of a Cardiganshire bench" *Ceredigion* (2004) xiv: 123. The Tucker Report is *Cmmd* 7061 (1947).

30 Lord Elwyn Jones, *In My Time: An Autobiography* (London: Weidenfeld and Nicolson Ltd., 1988) p. 136. He cites an occasion on which a juror asked to be excused on the grounds that his wife was "going to conceive that morning".

31 *The Times*, 5 February 1970.

32 *The Cambrian News and Merionethshire Standard*, 29 November 1918 (I am indebted to Gareth Bevan for this reference); Sir T. A. Jones, *Without My Wig* (Liverpool: Hugh Evans & Sons, 1944) pp. 166, 178–179, 185 and *The Union of England and Wales: A Reading* (London: Sir Isaac Pitman & Sons, 1937) pp. 23–31. For the 1967 Act, see *The Times*, 17 January 1972.

33 Johnes, *Wales Since 1939*, pp. 226–233; Davies, *Wales*, pp. 649–651.

34 *The Times*, 24, 28 April 1971. A refusal to complete census returns also was used as a measure of civil disobedience, one which had been tried long before, see R. Wallace, "'No votes for women, no information from women": the suffragette boycott of the 1911 census in Wales" *Llafur* (2013) 11: 56.

35 See D. Jenkins, *A Nation on Trial* (2nd edn, Cardiff: Welsh Academic Press, 1998); Davies, *Wales*, pp. 592–593, *The Times*, 9 September, 14 October, 8 December 1936.

36 The fullest description and analysis of the events of this and the following two paragraphs is to be found in J. Humphries, *Freedom Fighters: Wales's Forgotten*

War, 1963–1993 (Cardiff: University of Wales Press, 2008). See also N. Thomas, *The Welsh Extremist: A Culture in Crisis* (London: Lolfa, 1971). See also *The Times*, 24 December 1962.

37 NLW PE3986/138. I am grateful to Cymdeithas yr Iaith Cymraeg for their help in allowing me to make use of this source.

38 Humphries, *Freedom Fighters*, Chs 10–13; R. Williams (ed.), *Prison Letters: John Jenkins* (Talybont: Lolfa, 1981); J. Jenkins, "My battle for Wales" *Cambria* January/February 2009, p. 24.

39 Humphries, *Freedom Fighters*, Chs 15, 17 and Appendix A; see p. 166 for the quotation. Johnes, *Wales Since 1939*, pp. 385–387; Birch, *History of Policing*, Ch. XI.

40 Jones, *Crime and Policing*, pp. 23, 183.

41 P. Molloy, *Operation Seal Bay* (Llandysul: Gomer Press, 1986) p. 13; Johnes, *Wales Since 1939*, p. 107.

42 Birch, *Crime and Policing*, p. 341.

43 P. Davies, "The Probation Service in a rural area: problems and practicalities" in G. Dingwall and S. Moody (eds) *Crime and Conflict in the Countryside* (Cardiff: University of Wales Press, 1999) p. 146 at p. 154.

44 R. Taylor, *To Catch a Thief* (Chichester: New Wine Press, 2006) p. 58; P. Molloy, *Operation Seal Bay*, L. Ebenezer, *Operation Julie: The World's Greatest LSD Bust* (Talybont: Lolfa, 2010); Jones, *Crime and Policing*, p. 183–184.

45 K. Elliott Jones and W. Cope (eds), *The Swansea Wartime Diary of Laurie Latchford, 1940–1941* (Newport: South Wales Record Society, 2010) pp. 30, 38, 253; Jones, "Where did it all go wrong?" pp. 247, 249; Birch, *History of Policing*, p. 287.

46 See L. Koffman, *Crime Surveys and Victims of Crime* (Cardiff: University of Wales Press, 1996), "Key findings from the Aberystwyth Crime Survey" *Cambrian Law Review* (1997) 23: 33, "Crime in rural Wales" in G. Dingwall and S. Moody (eds) *Crime and Conflict*, p. 60.

47 *Cardigan and Tivy-Side Advertiser*, 5 March 1948; Emmet, *North Wales Village*, p. 77.

48 Ireland, "A second Ireland" pp. 247–9.

49 *The Times*, 17 November 1953, 17 March 1954. R. Davies (gol: L. Ebenezer), *Troseddau Hynod* (Llanrwst: Gwasg Carreg Gwalch, 2003) pp. 78–81. The photographs are in the Dyfed-Powys Police Museum collection.

50 S. Fielding, *The Executioner's Bible* (London: John Blake Publishing Ltd., 2008) Appendix.

51 See www.theguardian.com/uk-news/2013/sep/30/cardiff-three-inquiry-report; www.bbc.co.uk/news/uk-wales-south-east-wales-23329952.

52 See L. Ebenezer, *Frongoch and the Birth of the IRA* (Llanrwst: Gwasg Carreg Gwalch, 2006), S. McConville, *Irish Political Prisoners 1848–1922: Theatres of War* (London: Routledge, 2003) p. 643.

53 www.theguardian.com/news/datablog/2010/nov/08/prisoner-of-war-camps-uk#data; www.islandfarm.fsnet.co.uk/The%20Big%20Escape.htm.

54 See *Minutes of Evidence Taken before the Royal Commission on Wales and Monmouthshire* (London: Stationery Office, 1894), *Reformatory and Industrial Schoolboys sent to Welsh Farms 1910–1920*, TNA HO 45/10936/191433. I am indebted to Sue Passmore for drawing this to my attention.

55 See Appendix 2, Jones, *Crime and Policing*, pp. 46–51.

56 See www.lgcplus.com/walkout-as-welsh-mp-accuses-councils-of-corruption/1618267. article, *The Times*, 28 June 1974, 23 December 1975, Jones, *Crime and Policing*, p. 104.

57 Jones, *Crime and Policing*, p. 177.

58 For the release of the Jillings Report, see www.theguardian.com/uk-news/2013/jul/08/jillings-report-north-wales-child-abuse; for Waterhouse, see *Lost in Care: Report of the Tribunal of Inquiry into the Abuse of Children in Care in the Former County Council Areas of Gwynedd and Clwyd since 1974* (London: The Stationery Office, 2000).

Concluding remarks

The first of the Recommendations of the Waterhouse Report was for the establishment of an independent Children's Commissioner for Wales, and indeed such a post, the first in the UK, was created by Westminster legislation of 2001. By then, of course the first stage of Welsh devolved government had been attained. It should be noted more generally that the devolution settlement does not extend to matters of crime and punishment. Whether there will be further developments in the future, as suggested in relation to such matters as youth justice, policing and other such issues by the Silk Commission, in its report of 2014,[1] is beyond the scope of this book. The devolution settlement does, however, invite reflection on the nature of contemporary statehood. As the Introduction to this volume made clear, the narrative of the preceding five chapters has always been intimately connected to the concept of "state", in its existential, geographical and social dimensions. What has been learned? Has an account of crime and punishment in Wales anything important to offer in analytical terms, or have we simply seen a catalogue of local wonders, the equivalent of early printed topographical tour guides?

The search for a distinctively "Welsh" attitude towards criminality and the response to it is, in such simple terms, futile. Attitudes will vary over time, across social class, from area to area, farm to factory, Marcher Lord to *Meibion Glyndwr*. Such obvious complexity does not, however, mean that the Welsh experience can teach us nothing about the administration of criminal law, or indeed nothing extra which could not have been easily gathered by continuing to treat the experience of Wales simply as an adjunct to English criminal justice history. To the issue of state we will return in a moment, but let us pause briefly to consider demography, not as relating only to the history, but also the historiography of crime.

When I had written that last sentence I left my seat at Ceredigion Archives to call in at my dentist's surgery, perhaps 100 yards away, to confirm an appointment. On my way back I noticed, again, the faint residue of graffiti which had been subject to an official attempt at removal. The legend appears to take the form of a dispute as to whether a particular individual was or was not an "Aber grass snake". In conditions of urban anonymity I could not imagine such contention over a matter of "shame" (it needs hardly to be stated that the concept of "shame" in respect of, presumably, being a police informer, is a special and contestable one to which we must return) as productive of such public display, nor indeed of its having much purpose. Perhaps, subculturally, urban gangs might send out messages to their members, but, if the press is to be believed (it isn't always), then gangs have rather more direct forms of dealing with informers than by public proclamation. My point here is simply that where I live, in rural Wales, my notions of the present state of crime may not be the same as a dweller in an inner-city area. "We're all afraid of knife crime" declared a speaker at a conference I attended recently in the South-East of England. I wasn't, and said so. My point was not that I was lucky, that I could still leave my door unlocked as in some cosy invocation of a golden age, but that people who talk and write about criminality are, to an extent, creatures of their own cultural assumptions. We nowadays see crime through the lens of the urban because most writers on crime and its history are themselves dwellers in the urban. Quite why histories of crime and punishment tend to begin with the gravest and therefore most atypical examples, the execution rather than the bind-over or the fine, is a rather more intractable question. But the point remains an important one. Our historiography of crime and punishment is dominated by the urban, especially perhaps the metropolitan, and the grave. A survey of the long-term criminality of Wales may help us to question those starting points.

Does such questioning matter? I think that it does. Until 1851 more of the population of England and Wales lived outside towns rather than in them. The paradigm of the rural (or semi-rural, for these remain concepts with blurred edges) is an important one for many centuries before that, but it is one, I suggest, insufficiently embraced by many whose voices shape our understanding of the past. Let me give an example. Perhaps the most influential social theorist of the last half-century has been Michel Foucault, whose rich and insightful analyses have sparked a plethora of academic commentary. Foucault's brilliant work on the development of the "disciplinary gaze", translated into English as *Discipline and Punish*, which normalized and transformed social control away from the theatrical and corporeal and into the pervasive and psychological, should be read by all interested in the development of punishment and of the state. Yet in its contention that the locus of supervisory power was in the institution, specifically in this context in the Penitentiary, Foucault's work is profoundly unhistorical. The real triumph of the Victorian prison (the predecessors of which had, to illustrate the other failing of much contemporary historiography, been routinely dealing with less serious breaches of the criminal law for centuries) was not the creation of the disciplinary gaze, but its attempt to refashion it for a newly urban society. The crisis for traditional methods of social control is not something which is revealed only to the modern social theorist, but was recognized even as the prison walls were being erected. As Matthew Davenport Hill put it in 1852:

> I think it will not require any long train of reflection to show that in small towns there must be a sort of natural police, of a very wholesome kind, operating on the conduct of every individual, who lives, as it were, under the public eye. But in a large town, he lives, as it were, in absolute obscurity.[2]

Although, as has been shown, major industrial changes, particularly in the nineteenth century, did alter the demographic character of particular parts of Wales, they did not wholly expunge, indeed they to an extent imported, an older tradition. To begin to study crime in Wales is to start from a position in which much of the history of criminality occurred in communities in which people knew each other's business. It also is to accept that, unexciting as it may seem, the minor theft or brawl, rather than the horrible murder, is the historically normal, rather than the analytically secondary, or atypical. For what it's worth, I take this to be the case for other jurisdictions too, but I can't guarantee that I would if I were writing a history of the criminal justice system in England from an urban university centre.

Such personal reflections might explain my own stance, but they do not, on their own, justify a book which contains more than enough savage murders and mass rioting. If the criminal history of Wales is to operate as more than a grisly gazetteer, we must look to the wider truths which it suggests. To do so will involve investigation at a very basic (not simple, far from it, but basic) level. We need to consider issues which were exposed in the earliest period considered within this book: What is the nature of "crime" and what is the role of "state"?

All societies possess certain rules by which social interaction is guided and expectations of acceptable conduct are underwritten. The very idea of a rule carries with it the idea of liability to a sanction if there is an infraction. We tend to reserve the term "criminal law" for those rules which represent general public standards, formulated and enforced by state agencies. It is unwise to be too dogmatic here, for Chapter 1 has pointed out that custom may exist without a single "legislative" origin, nor does the fact that the punitive power lies in the hands of private individuals such as the victim or the victim's kin necessarily mean that the wrong is an entirely personal one, with no greater social dimension. However that may be, the essence of such social rules is to protect the security of interests considered essential: religion, honour, body and property originally, but the list will vary, and expand, over time. The hidden problem in this analysis is to identify what we mean by the "society" which is governed by these "social" rules.

As mentioned, the term "criminal" applies most easily when the society in question is the state. We have seen in Chapter 1 that in the world of feud and compensation the state acts, at most, as a background against which rule breach is addressed, a framer of appropriate response rather than its agency. Chapter 2 has shown us that in Wales the concept of state is a developing and contingent one, in which more or less autonomous lordships are overtaken by conquest and assimilation to form part of a greater territorial, bureaucratic and juridical entity. In our own time the paradigmatic "society" is the nation state, a fact paradoxically confirmed by debates over independence within the UK or relations with European Union. The state is our default society, others – the football club, the Women's Institute – we join through choice. And the state is our default righter of wrongs: "Have you reported it?" we ask anxiously, on hearing of a theft or assault.

But if we change the term "society" in our analysis and substitute the word "community", then we begin to understand some of the tensions which the second half of the book has explored. For the state is there shown to be one community amongst several: the village, the chapel, the industry (though not any industry: we talk of "mining communities", but not, generally, of "car-making communities" or "information technology communities"). What is being worked out in the latter part of this book is the extent to which the state can or should assume dominance over these other communities in respect of the rectification of wrongdoing. When we accept that social markers of a community include such matters as language, custom and religion, we may hypothesize that Wales might prove more resistant to that dominance, although not universally and uniformly so, than if such variables coincided with those of the nation state. Where the attitudes of state are found to be in opposition to those of other communities, over tithes, or industrial disputes for example, we might expect that tension to be dramatically highlighted. But competing normative orders do not always have to clash so overtly as in such instances; they may compete quietly, even unacknowledged, at the level of individual responses to individual events. The question remains as to the claims of which "community", which normative order, are to be the more important, more appropriate or more effective.

There is a further dynamic, the issue of "What works?" Prosecution, trial and punishment may be one response to wrongdoing, but the victim and the victim's family or neighbours ("the community" in this instance) may have no incentive to go to trouble or expense of invoking a distant and different power to obtain redress. If compensation, or ostracism or shaming have proved effective methods of restoring social harmony in the past, then why should they not in the present? This is particularly the case in those areas in which social change has been relatively slow and undramatic. I am not suggesting for a moment that a farmer's life in a small upland hamlet is the same in 1950 as it was in 1850, still less 1450, but I am suggesting that, despite the historian's desire to find changes and fresh starts, elements of continuity may still survive, and "what worked before" might remain a valid response to rule breach.

None of this is to take a romantic view of the past, in which a traditional, Welsh (and Welsh-speaking) peasantry pause on the way back from an Eisteddfod to administer traditional justice towards a malefactor, whilst looking over their shoulder to avoid the clumsy, alien state apparatus of an distant and uncomprehending power. The discussion in the previous chapters has shown that the "traditional" may be violent, prejudiced and supportive of an inequitable social order. The Carmarthenshire woman driven to suicide from shame in 1851 presumably felt she had reason to fear "community" judgment, as did the farm servant girls who hid their pregnancies and killed their infants.[3] My purpose here is analytical rather than evaluative. I want to explain some of the characteristics of the history of crime and punishment in Wales rather than excuse or mourn a lost paradise.

The ideas of "community" and the techniques of state intervention continue to evolve. As to the former, social networking means that our understanding of the notion, now freed from geographical restraint, are being reconsidered, whilst global communications iron out, to an extent, local particularities. As to state intervention in criminality, it too moves on from the Victorian "day in court" to concepts of surveillance, increased use of cautions and offender registers. Historians in the future will have different things to say about crime and punishment in Wales, and maybe other historians of criminality would have other, better, things to say than those within this book. My aim has been a limited one, however. I hope that the history of Welsh criminal justice will receive more attention, from those outside Wales as well as from those within it, than it has to date. I hope that those who continue to ignore it will not be able to do so without feeling some discomfort.

Notes

1 See Legislative Powers to Strengthen Wales, 2014, Ch. 10, http://commissionondevoluti oninwales.independent.gov.uk/files/2014/03/Empowerment-Responsibility-Legislative-Po wers-to-strengthen-Wales.pdf.
2 Quoted in Y. Levin and A. Lindesmith, "English ecology and criminology of the past century" *Journal of Criminal Law and Criminology* (1927): 801 at p. 804.
3 See Ireland, *Want of Order*, pp. 66–72, "Perhaps my mother murdered me" *passim.* I contemplated including here the case of the Gwent paediatrician who had her house daubed in 2000 by those who thought the term equated to "paedophile", but the case, though it did happen, has had its significance overstated, see www.pressga zette.co.uk/wire/8897.

Appendix I

The introduction of the "New Police" into Wales

I list below the foundation dates, where known, for the County and Borough Police Forces within Wales. Later amalgamations and reconstitutions of forces (e.g. Dyfed-Powys Police) are not given here, although Chapter 5 of this book does discuss more modern restructuring. This information is abstracted for the most part from M. Stallion and D.S. Wall, *The British Police: Forces and Chief Officers 1829–2012* (2nd edn, Hook, 2011) Ch. 5. I depart from their dating at some points, e.g. they give 1827 as the date for Carmarthen Borough, which must be an error (not least from the book's title!) and both Jones (*Crime in Wales*) and the South Wales Police themselves (at their Museum website www.southwalespolicemuseum.org.uk/en/content/cms/history_of_the_force/history_of_the_force.aspx) give 1841 for the foundation of the Glamorgan force, rather than 1839. There is also a problem with the dating of the Merthyr Tydfil force. I have listed the rest mostly from Stallion and Wall, though I confess that I have not checked every force myself and have footnoted alternative datings (principally from the list in H.K. Birch, *History of Policing in North Wales* at p. 61). Some difficulties arise since, for example, old borough forces might receive a new Head Constable, sometimes from the Metropolitan Police, to preside over their constables before a force on a "new" basis was established.[1] I might have hoped to find these datings more uniformly given in my sources, but my aim here is simply to give an indication of developments, the task of researching each force independently for this list was too daunting to be attempted for a work of this nature.

Note the important dates of particular Acts which are significant in this process: The Municipal Corporations Act 1835, The Rural Constabulary Act 1839 and The County and Borough Police Act 1856, for a discussion of the provisions of which (and other related legislation) see, e.g., P. Rawlings, *Policing: A Short History*, Chs 5 and 6. More than half of the forces listed here have books or articles relating to their history. Some of these are quoted in the notes to the text in this book, but I am spared the necessity of a full bibliography again by the work of Stallion and Wall, which does provide references relating to particular forces. South Wales Police Museum has an attractive and informative website which gives much information on the history of the force and its constituent predecessors. Those desirous of details relating to individual forces are advised to cross-refer to this literature for details.

Aberystwyth 1837
Anglesey 1857
Beaumaris 1836
Brecon 1829
Breconshire 1857
Bridgend 1838
Caernarvonshire 1857
Cardiff 1836
Cardiganshire 1844
Carmarthen 1836[2]
Carmarthenshire 1843
Denbigh 1854[3]
Denbighshire 1840
Dowlais 1832[4]
Flint 1836[5]
Flintshire 1856
Glamorgan 1839
Haverfordwest 1835[6]
Kidwelly 1857
Merionethshire 1857
Merthyr Tydfil 1908[7]
Mold 1841
Monmouth 1836
Monmouthshire 1857
Montgomeryshire 1840
Neath 1836[8]
Newport (Mons) 1836
Pembroke 1836[9]
Pembrokeshire 1857
Pwllheli 1857
Radnorshire 1857
Swansea 1836
Tenby 1840[10]
Welshpool 1835?[11]

Notes

1 Jones, *Crime in Wales*, p. 204.
2 Birch and also Griffiths (*Heddluoedd*) give 1831. I rely for 1836 on Spurrell, *Carmarthen* and Molloy *Shilling for Carmarthen*.
3 "?" in Stallion and Wall.
4 No separate force given in Birch or South Wales Police.
5 From Birch, c.1835 in Stallion and Wall.

6 Birch: 1833.
7 Stallion and Wall give "1831?", but Birch gives 1908 and South Wales Police give the same, policing before then being by "A" Division of the Glamorgan County Force.
8 Birch and South Wales Police. Not in Stallion and Wall.
9 Birch, p. 186.
10 Birch, "c.1840" in Stallion and Wall.
11 "?" in Birch.

Appendix II
Wales and the prison

For the enthusiastic historian of prisons, Wales offers some splendid sites of interest. As well as museum displays, including one in the old police cells at Carmarthen, there are two preserved County Gaols which may be visited, in Beaumaris on Anglesey and Ruthin in Denbighshire. In addition the charming market town of Montgomery has, with its castle gatehouse, two later prisons and a House of Correction, possibly the most impressive, and attractive, concentration of penal provision in Britain. Details of particular institutions, their staff and inmate populations, are now rather easier to discover than once they were; the nineteenth-century Prison Inspectors Reports will be available online to readers with access to the British Parliamentary Papers site, whilst individual volumes and articles have been produced relating information about individual gaols and their inmates.[1] Local newspapers often reproduce extracts from Inspectors' Reports concerning their own "gaol" and sometimes are more inclusive in their coverage, as in *The Cambrian News* article on "The Prisons of Wales" of 23 August 1872.

The figures below are abstracted from John Howard's seminal *The State of The Prisons* of 1777 and show the number of prisoners, both debtors and felons, in Welsh gaols and Houses of Correction inspected by Howard. Figures are given for 1776 and also given in brackets for 1774 where Howard records them, and other dates of inspection are given as appropriate. I have retained his spelling. A dash indicates that no figures are provided in his survey.

By contrast (the contrast is necessarily one of impression; the figures do not relate to the same things) in the year 1876 a total of 6,486 persons were committed to Welsh prisons. On 29 September 1876 there were 166 prisoners in Cardiff Gaol, of whom only 4 were debtors.[2] Impressionistic in their conclusions as they are, the figures leave no doubt as to the general nature of the "penal revolution" discussed in the text.

Prison closures became easier after nationalization had severed the essential link with the individual counties. Aberystwyth Borough Gaol was closed by the 1865 Act, whilst the following were closed under the 1877 Act: Beaumaris, Brecon (reopened 1880), Cardigan, Mold, Dolgellau, Montgomery, Haverfordwest, Presteigne. Later closures were Brecon (1916), Ruthin (1916), Carmarthen (1922), Caernarfon (1922) and Usk (1922–1939).[3]

Table A2.1 The number of prisoners, both debtors and felons, in Welsh gaols and
Houses of Correction inspected by Howard

Institution	Total prisoners	Debtors	Felons etc
Monmouth	15 (22)	6 (10)	9 (12)
Usk Bridewell	3 (2)	-	-
Flint	0	0	0
Ruthin	3 (13)	2 (8)	1 (5)
Wrexham Bridewell	1 (2)	-	-
Montgomery	2 (in 1775)	2	0
Montgomery Bridewell	0 (in 1775)	0	0
Beaumaris	2 (in 1774)	2	0
Carnarvon	3 (in 1774)	2	1
Dolgelley	2 (in 1774)	1	1
Cardigan	4 (in 1774)	4	0
Haverfordwest	5 (in 1774)	4	1
Haverfordwest Town	0 (in 1774)	0	0
Carmarthen	11 (26)	4 (16)	7 (10)
Carmarthen Borough	4 (1)	3 (0)	1 (1)
Presteign	4 (7)	3 (4)	1 (3)
Brecon	5 (10)	4 (7)	1 (3)
Brecon Bridewell	0	0	0
Brecon Town Gaol	0	0	0
Cardiff	4 (16)	2 (14)	2 (2)
Cowbridge	0 (0)	0 (0)	0 (0)
Total	68	39	25

Note: Total covers one survey from each gaol
Source: J. Howard *The State of the Prisons* (reprint, Abingdon: Routledge, 1977)

Notes

1 See, for example, my own *Want of Order*, based around, but not restricted to, the
gaol at Carmarthen, the two volumes of Ireland and Ireland, *The Carmarthen
Gaoler's Journal 1845–50*, and the searchable database of prisoners at the Welsh
Legal History Society website at www.welshlegalhistory.org/carms-felons-register.
php. Carmarthen has also attracted a volume, *The Black Flag over Carmarthen* by
P. Goodall (Llanrwst: Llygad Gwalch Cyf, 2005) who has also produced other
popular histories *Down Through the Trap Door: The History of Monmouth and Usk
Gaols* (Llanrwst: Llygad Gwalch Cyf, 2010) and *Ring the Bell in the Gaols of Brecon
"Canwch y Gloch"* (Llanrwst: Llygad Gwalch Cyf 2006). Beaumaris has M.
Hughes, *Crime and Punishment at Beaumaris* (Llanrwst: Llygad Gwalch Cyf,
2006), Ch. 1 of Davies's *Law and Disorder* deals with Brecon County Gaol, whilst
Montgomery is discussed in A. and J. Welton, *The Story of Montgomery*, Ch. 12
(and, in a rather nice contemporary review of the newly built gaol, in S. Lewis,
Topographical Dictionary of Wales vol II (1833)). Usk is served by B. Foster "The

Usk houses of correction and the early days of Usk county gaol" *Gwent Local History* 94 (2003): 3.

2 For the figures, see Jones, *Crime in Wales*, p. 230, R.W. Ireland, "Reflections on a silent system" in T.G. Watkin (ed.) *The Garthbeibio Murders and Other Essays* (Bangor: Welsh Legal History Society, 2007) p. 65.

3 See A. Brodie, J. Croom and J. Davies, *English Prisons [sic]: An Architectural History* (Swindon: English Heritage, 2002) Appendices 2 and 3.

Select bibliography

I am always excited by the thought of producing a bibliography, even though it is an element of a book which is used selectively, if at all. I am particularly interested in the coded messages which bibliographies contain, the author seeking to include as many works as he or she can, to display the immense breadth of their reading (even perhaps when not all of the books have been read), or to overemphasize the significance of their own contributions by citing even the most ephemeral of their own publications. Bibliographies, then, ostensibly written for the benefit of the reader, may be readily used to magnify the reputation of the writer.

I am willing to admit to drawing a number of my own works, but not too many, to the reader's attention in what follows below; times are hard and the ACLS photocopying royalty often proves a lifeline. I may not have read every last word of every chapter of every tome cited, though I have read the vast bulk. But I should explain the principles I have applied here. I am, perhaps, assuming a reader more interested in the history of crime and punishment than of Wales, so my emphasis is on the former rather than on more general historical accounts, though some of the latter are included, particularly where they give helpful context or points of reference. I have tried to include alongside the standard academic studies a number of more popular works, both because in truth it is difficult to draw a clear line between them (where does this book fall? It contains the fruit of many years study, but I hope that it may be enjoyed by the general reader) and also because I want to give the reader a sense of the width and vitality of the interest in these matters in Wales. Essentially, I suppose, I want to say to the historians of crime in England "How dare you ignore this stuff? There's such wealth in it!". Whilst some of the studies here may lack a focus or context which might be expected in scholarly tomes, they often contain the fruits of great industry in local archives or newspaper collections. Yet I have not included all the local town or county histories, all the various diaries or travellers' accounts which have provided information and which appear in the footnotes. Nor have I included here any of the primary archival resources which are available only in specific locations, since they will not be easy to access for many readers. The same applies to other unpublished material or that which, like Parliamentary

Papers, may not be easily accessible to the general reader. Again, these are referenced in the footnotes. I have provided below a few website references which overcome this difficulty. After some thought I have decided to give only names of these, rather than complex and potentially mutable URLs (again, these are given in the footnotes) since I suspect that most people will find entering these into a search engine easier and more reliable than attempting to transcribe often complex and meaningless series of strokes and letters.

Websites

Archival repositories such as County Archives and the National Library of Wales have, of course, their own websites which contain detailed information on their particular holdings. The following have also been of use in writing this volume.

Archives Network Wales
Canolfan Hywel Dda Centre
Dyfed-Powys Police Museum and Archive
Gwefan Cyfraith Hywel Website
House of Commons British Parliamentary Papers
National Library of Wales Crime and Punishment (Great Sessions) Database
National Library of Wales Welsh Newspapers Online Database
South Wales Police Museum
The Judges Lodging, Presteigne
Welsh Legal History Society

Books and articles

Ashton, O. "Chartism in Llanidloes: the riot of 1839 revisited" *Llafur* 10 (2010): 76.
Bartlett, R. *The Hanged Man* (Princeton, NJ: Princeton University Press, 2004).
Beddoe, D. "Carmarthenshire women and criminal transportation to Australia 1787–1852" *The Carmarthenshire Antiquary* 13 (1974): 65.
Beddoe, D. *Welsh Convict Women* (Barry: S. Williams, 1979).
Birch, H.C. *The History of Policing in North Wales* (Pwllheli: Gwasg Carreg Gwalch, 2008).
Bowen, I. *The Statutes of Wales* (London: T.F. Unwin, 1908).
Bruley, S. *The Women and Men of 1926: A Gender and Social History of the General Strike and Miners' Lockout in South Wales* (Cardiff: University of Wales Press, 2010).
Bush, K. "The labour of Sisyphus – Dafydd Jenkins and the National Petition on the Welsh Language" in N. Cox and T. Watkin (eds) *Canmlwyddiant*, p. 42.
Carradice, P. *Nautical Training Ships: An Illustrated History* (Stroud: Amberley Publishing, 2009).
Chapman, M. "A sixteenth-century trial for felony in the Court of Great Sessions for Montgomeryshire" *The Montgomeryshire Collections* 78 (1990): 167.
Chapman, M. (ed.) *Criminal Proceedings in the Montgomeryshire Court of Great Sessions: Transcript of Commonwealth Gaol Files 1650–1660* (Aberystwyth: National Library of Wales, 1996).

Chapman, M. (ed.) *The Montgomery Court of Great Sessions* (Aberystwyth: National Library of Wales, vols from 2004, 2008, 2010).

Chapman, M. "Life in Montgomeryshire during the Tudor and Stuart periods" in *National Library of Wales Journal* xxxv, 2 (2011): 70.

Charles-Edwards, T. *The Welsh Laws* (Cardiff: University of Wales Press, 1989).

Charles-Edwards, T. "The Galanas tractate in Iorwerth: texts and legal development" in T. Charles-Edwards and P. Russell (eds) *Tair Colofn Cyfraith/ The Three Columns of Law in Medieval Wales: Homicide, Theft and Fire* (Bangor: The Welsh Legal History Society, 2005) p. 92.

Charles-Edwards, T. "The Welsh law of theft: Iorwerth versus the rest" in T. Charles-Edwards and P. Russell (eds) *Tair Colofn Cyfraith/ The Three Columns of Law in Medieval Wales: Homicide, Theft and Fire* (Bangor: The Welsh Legal History Society, 2005) p. 108.

Charles-Edwards, T. *Wales and the Britons 350–1064* (Oxford: Oxford University Press, 2013).

Chase, M. "Rethinking Welsh Chartism" *Llafur* 10 (2010): 39.

Clement, M. *Correspondence and Minutes of the SPCK Relating to Wales 1699–1740* (Cardiff: University of Wales Press, 1952).

Clements, F. "Female crime and punishment in nineteenth century Denbighshire" *Denbighshire Historical Society Transactions* 60 (2012): 95.

Clwyd R.O. *The Mold Riots* (Clwyd: Clwyd Record Office, 1991).

Cooke, N. "*The King v Richard Lewis and Lewis Lewis* (Cardiff, 13 July 1831): the trial of Dic Penderyn" in T. Watkin (ed.) *The Trial of Dic Penderyn and Other Essays* (Cardiff: The Welsh Legal History Society, 2002) p. 110.

Davies, D. *Law and Disorder in Breconshire 1750–1880* (Brecon: Evans).

Davies, I. "The last time 'justice' was seen to be done: the fate of Matthew Francis of Newport" *Gwent Local History* 106 (2009): 36.

Davies, J. *A History of Wales* (London: Penguin, 1993).

Davies, P. "The Probation Service in a rural area: problems and practicalities" in G. Dingwall and S. Moody (eds) *Crime and Conflict in the Countryside* (Cardiff: University of Wales Press, 1999) p. 146.

Davies, Roy (gol: L. Ebenezer) *Troseddau Hynod* (Llanrwst: Gwasg Correg Gwalch, 2003).

Davies, R.R. "The twilight of Welsh Law 1284–1536" *History* li (1966): 143.

Davies, R.R. "The survival of the bloodfeud in medieval Wales" *History* 54 (1969): 338.

Davies, R.R. *Lordship and Society in the March of Wales 1282–1400* (Oxford: Oxford University Press, 1978).

Davies, R.R. *The Revolt of Owain Glyn Dŵr* (Oxford: Oxford University Press, 1997).

Davies, Russell. "'In a broken dream': some aspects of sexual behaviour and the dilemmas of the unmarried mother in South West Wales, 1887–1914" *Llafur* 3 (1983): 24.

Davies, Russell. *Secret Sins: Sex, Violence and Society in Carmarthenshire 1870–1920* (Cardiff: University of Wales Press, 1996).

Davies, W. *Wales in the Early Middle Ages* (Leicester: Leicester University Press, 1982).

"Demos" "The Welsh magistracy" *The Welsh Outlook* xix (1932): 204.

Denbighshire Archives. *Enrolling the Past: A Description of Denbighshire Quarter Sessions Rolls, 1706–1800* (CD-Rom, Denbigh, 2003).

Dimmock, S. "Social conflict in Welsh towns c. 1280–1530" in H. Fulton (ed.) *Urban Culture in Medieval Wales* (Cardiff: University of Wales Press, 2012) p. 117.

Dubé, S. (ed.) *My Failings and Imperfections: The Diary of Rees Thomas of Dôl-llan, 1860–1862* (Llandybie: Carmarthenshire Antiquarian Society, 2011).

Ebenezer, L. *Frongoch and the Birth of the IRA* (Llanrwst: Gwasg Correg Gwalch, 2006).

Ebenezer, L. *Operation Julie: The World's Greatest LSD Bust* (Talybont: Lolfa, 2010).

Elliott Jones, K. and Cope, W. (eds) *The Swansea Wartime Diary of Laurie Latchford, 1940–1941* (Newport: South Wales Record Society, 2010).

Ellis Jones, M. "'The confusion of Babel'? The Welsh language, law courts and legislation in the nineteenth century" in G. Jenkins (ed.) *The Welsh Language and its Social Domains 1801–1911* (Cardiff: University of Wales Press, 2000) p. 587.

Ellis, B. "The conveyance of vagrants across Montgomeryshire 1787–1806" in *Montgomeryshire Collections* 98 (2010): 55.

Elwyn Jones, Lord. *In My Time: An Autobiography* (London: Weidenfeld and Nicolson Ltd., 1988).

Emmet, I. *A North Wales Village: A Social Anthropological Study* (London: Routledge, 1964).

Evans, G. and Maddox, D. *The Tonypandy Riots 1910–1911* (Plymouth: University of Plymouth Press, 2010).

Evans, N. "The urbanization of Welsh society" in T. Herbert and G.E. Jones (eds) *People and Protest: Wales 1815–1850* (Cardiff: University of Wales Press, 1988) p. 7.

Foster, B. "The Usk houses of correction and the early days of Usk county gaol" *Gwent Local History* 94 (2003): 3.

Francis, H. "The law, oral tradition and the mining community" *Journal of Law and Society* 12 (1985): 267.

Goodall, P. *For Whom the Bell Tolls: Executions at Swansea Prison* (Llandysul: Gomer Press, 2001).

Goodall, P. *The Black Flag over Carmarthen* (Llanrwst: Llygad Gwalch Cyf, 2005).

Goodall, P. *Ring the Bell in the Gaols of Brecon "Canwch y Gloch"* (Llanrwst: Llygad Gwalch Cyf, 2006).

Goodall, P. *Down Through the Trap Door: The History of Monmouth and Usk Gaols* (Llanrwst: Llygad Gwalch Cyf, 2010).

Griffith, W. *Power, Politics and County Government in Wales: Anglesey 1780–1914* (Llangefni: Anglesey Antiquarian Society, 2006).

Griffiths, C. *Heddluoedd Canolbarth a Gorllewin Cymru 1829–1974/ The Police Forces of Mid and West Wales* (Llandybie: Dinefwr Publishers, 2008).

Harding, C. and Ireland, R.W. *Punishment: Rhetoric, Rule and Practice* (London: Routledge, 1989).

Henriques, U. "The Jews and crime in South Wales before World War I" *Morgannwg* xxix (1985): 59.

Herbert, T. and Jones, G.E. (eds) *People and Protest: Wales 1815–1850* (Cardiff: University of Wales Press, 1988).

Hopkin, D. "The Llanelli Riots 1911" *History Review* 11 (1983): 488.

Hopkins, T. "Quarter sessions and the justice of the peace in Monmouthshire" *The Monmouthshire Antiquary* xxix (2013): 47.

Howard, J. *The State of the Prisons* (1777, repr. Abingdon: Routledge, 1977).

Howard, S. "Riotous community: crowds, politics and society in Wales, c.1700–1840" *The Welsh History Review* 20 (2001): 656.

Howard, S. "Investigating responses to theft in early modern Wales: communities, thieves and the courts" *Continuity and Change* 19 (2004): 409.

Howard, S. *Law and Disorder in Early Modern Wales: Crime and Authority in the Denbighshire Courts, c.1660–1730* (Cardiff: University of Wales Press, 2008).

Howell, D. "The Rebecca Riots" in T. Herbert and G.E. Jones (eds) *People and Protest: Wales 1815–1850* (Cardiff: University of Wales Press, 1988) p. 113.

Howell, D. *The Rural Poor in Eighteenth-Century Wales* (Cardiff: University of Wales Press, 2000).

Hughes, D. "The effect of infrastructure development on crime in rural areas: a case study of the A55 Coastal Expressway in North Wales" *Cambrian Law Review* 27 (1996): 33.

Hughes, M. *Crime and Punishment at Beaumaris* (Llanrwst: Llygad Gwalch Cyf, 2006).

Humphreys, M. *The Crisis of Community: Montgomeryshire, 1680–1815* (Cardiff: University of Wales Press, 1996).

Humphries, J. *Freedom Fighters: Wales's Forgotten War, 1963–1993* (Cardiff: University of Wales Press, 2008).

Ireland, R.W. "Eugene Buckley and the diagnosis of insanity in the early Victorian prison" *Llafur* 6 (1993): 5.

Ireland, R.W. "Confinement with hard labour: motherhood and penal practice in a Victorian gaol" *Welsh History Review* 18 (1997): 621.

Ireland, R.W. "'An increasing mass of heathens in the bosom of a Christian land': the railway and crime in the nineteenth century" *Continuity and Change* 12 (1997): 55.

Ireland, R.W. "Putting oneself on whose country? Carmarthenshire juries in the mid-nineteenth century" in T.G. Watkin (ed.) *Legal Wales: Its Past, Its Future* (Cardiff: Welsh Legal History Society, 2001) p. 63.

Ireland, R.W. "Law in action, law in books: the practicality of medieval theft law" *Continuity and Change* 17 (2002): 309.

Ireland, R.W. "The felon and the angel copier: criminal identity and the promise of photography in Victorian England and Wales" in L. Knafla (ed.) *Policing and War in Europe* (Westport, CT: Greenwood Press, 2002) p. 53.

Ireland, R.W. "Caught on camera: Cardiganshire's criminal portraits in context" *Ceredigion* xv (2006): 11.

Ireland, R.W. *"A Want of Order and Good Discipline": Rules, Discretion and the Victorian Prison* (Cardiff: University of Wales Press, 2007).

Ireland, R.W. "'A second Ireland'? Crime and popular culture in nineteenth-century Wales" in R. McMahon (ed.) *Crime, Law and Popular Culture in Europe, 1500–1900* (Cullompton: Willan, 2008) p. 239.

Ireland, R.W. "Sanctity, superstition and the death of Sarah Jacob" in A. Musson and C. Stebbings (eds) *Making Legal History: Approaches and Methodologies* (Cambridge: Cambridge University Press, 2012) p. 284.

Ireland, R.W. and Ireland, R.I. (eds) *The Carmarthen Gaoler's Journal 1845–1850* (2 vols, Bangor: Welsh Legal History Society, 2010).

Jenkins, D. *Hywel Dda: The Law* (Llandysul: Gomer Press, 1986).

Jenkins, D. *A Nation on Trial* (2nd edn, Cardiff: Welsh Academic Press, 1998).

Jenkins, D. "Crime and tort and the three columns of law" in T. Charles-Edwards and P. Russell (eds) *Tair Colofn Cyfraith: The Three Columns of Law in Medieval Wales* (Bangor: The Welsh Legal History Society, 2005) p. 1.

Jenkins, G. *The Foundations of Modern Wales 1642–1780* (Oxford: Oxford University Press, 1993).

Jenkins, J. "My battle for Wales" *Cambria* January/February (2009): 24.

Jenkins, P. *A History of Modern Wales 1536–1990* (London: Routledge, 1992).

Johnes, M. *Wales Since 1939* (Manchester: Manchester University Press, 2012).

Johnson, L. "Attitudes towards spousal violence in medieval Wales" *Welsh History Review* 24 (2009): 81.

Jones, D.J.V. *Before Rebecca: Popular Protests in Wales 1793–1835* (London: Allen Lane, 1973).

Jones, D.J.V. "A dead loss to the community: the criminal vagrant in mid-nineteenth-century Wales" *Welsh History Review* 8 (1977): 312.

Jones, D.J.V. *The Last Rising: The Newport Insurrection of 1839* (Oxford: Oxford University Press, 1985).

Jones, D.J.V. "Scotch cattle and Chartism" in T. Herbert and G.E. Jones (eds) *People and Protest: Wales 1815–1850* (Cardiff: University of Wales Press, 1988) p. 139.

Jones, D.J.V. *Rebecca's Children* (Oxford: Oxford University Press, 1989).

Jones, D.J.V. "Rebecca, crime and policing: a turning point in nineteenth-century attitudes" *Transactions of the Honourable Society of Cymmrodorion* (1990): 99.

Jones, D.J.V. "Where did it all go wrong? Crime in Swansea 1938–68" *Welsh History Review* 15 (1990): 240.

Jones, D.J.V. *Crime in Nineteenth-Century Wales* (Cardiff: University of Wales Press, 1992).

Jones, D.J.V. *Crime and Policing in the Twentieth Century: The South Wales Experience* (Cardiff: University of Wales Press, 1996) p. 287.

Jones, D.L. "A death at Borth in 1894: the capture, trial and execution of Thomas Richards" *Ceredigion* xvi (2010): 11.

Jones, Dot. *Statistical Evidence relating to the Welsh Language 1801–1911* (Cardiff: University of Wales Press, 1998).

Jones, J.G. *Wales and the Tudor State* (Cardiff: University of Wales Press, 1989).

Jones, J.G. *Early Modern Wales, c.1525–1640* (Basingstoke: Palgrave Macmillan, 1994).

Jones, J.G. *Law, Order and Government in Caernarfonshire 1558–1640* (Cardiff: University of Wales Press, 1996).

Jones, J.G. "The Welsh language and local government: Justices of the Peace and the Courts of Quarter Sessions c.1536–1800" in G. Jenkins (ed.) *The Welsh Language Before the Industrial Revolution* (Cardiff: University of Wales Press, 1997) p. 181.

Jones, K. *Alas! Poor Heslop: The Last Fatal Duel in Wales* (Cardigan: Summerhill Press, 2007).

Jones, M. "Rural and industrial protest in North Wales" in T. Herbert and G.E. Jones (eds) *People and Protest: Wales 1815–1850* (Cardiff: University of Wales Press, 1988) p. 165.

Jones, Rachael. "Three legal cases from the history of the Gregynog estate" in T.G. Watkin (ed.) *The Carno Poisonings and Other Essays* (Bangor: Welsh Legal Society, 2013) p. 121.

Jones, Rhian E. "Symbol, ritual and popular protest in early nineteenth-century Wales: the Scotch cattle rebranded" *Welsh History Review* 26 (2012): 34.

Jones, Richard. "The strange case of a wartime pig and a judicial inquiry into the conduct of a Cardiganshire bench" *Ceredigion* xiv (2004): 12.

Jones, Rosemary. "Popular culture, policing and the disappearance of the Ceffyl Pren in Cardiganshire c.1837–1850" *Ceredigion* 11 (1989–1992): 19.

Jones, Rosemary. "Women, community and collective action: the Ceffyl Pren Tradition" in A. John (ed.) *Our Mothers' Land: Chapters in Welsh Women's History 1830–1939* (Cardiff: University of Wales Press, 1991): p. 17.

Jones, Sir T. A. *The Union of England and Wales: A Reading* (London: Sir Isaac Pitman & Sons, 1937).

Jones, Sir T. A. *Without My Wig* (Liverpool: Hugh Evans & Sons, 1944).

Jones, T. *Rioting in North East Wales 1536–1918* (Wrexham: Bridge Books, 1997).

Jones-Parry, S.H. "Crime in Wales" *The Red Dragon* III (1888): 522.

Jukes, T. "'Mary the cripple': the Yarwood family's life of crime and vice in Victorian South Wales" *Gwent Local History* 111 (2012): 18.

Koffman, L. *Crime Surveys and Victims of Crime* (Cardiff: University of Wales Press, 1996).

Koffman, L. "Key findings from the Aberystwyth Crime Survey" *Cambrian Law Review* 23 (1997): 33.

Koffman, L. "Crime in rural Wales" in G. Dingwall, and S. Moody (eds) *Crime and Conflict in the Countryside* (Cardiff: University of Wales Press, 1999) p. 60.

Lewis, T.H. "Documents illustrating the County Gaol and House of Correction in Wales" in *Transactions of the Honourable Society of Cymmrodorion, Session 1946–47* (1948): 232.

Little, L.K. "Spiritual sanctions in Wales" in R. Blumenfeld-Kosinski and T. Szell (eds) *Images of Sainthood in Medieval Europe* (Ithaca, NY: Cornell University Press, 1991) p. 67.

Lloyd-Jones, H. "The Glanareth murder" in *Transactions of the Honourable Society of Cymmrodorion* (1948): 271.

Löffler, M. *Welsh Responses to the French Revolution: Press and Public Discourse 1989–1802* (Cardiff: University of Wales Press, 2012).

Lost in Care: Report of the Tribunal of Inquiry into the Abuse of Children in Care in the Former County Council Areas of Gwynedd and Clwyd since 1974 (London: Stationery Office, 2000).

McIlroy, J., Campbell, A. and Gildart, K. *Industrial Politics and the 1926 Mining Lockout: The Struggle for Dignity* (Cardiff: University of Wales Press, 2009).

Maddox, W.C. *A History of the Radnorshire Constabulary* (Llandrindod Wells: Radnorshire Society, 1959).

Matthias, K. "The Mad Irishman's Letter" *Clwyd Historian* 64 (2011).

Molloy, P. *And They Blessed Rebecca* (Llandysul: Gomer Press, 1983).

Molloy, P. *Operation Seal Bay* (Llandysul: Gomer Press, 1986).

Molloy, P. *A Shilling for Carmarthen … The Town They Nearly Tamed* (Fishguard: Gomer Press, 1991).

Morris, M.G.R. (ed.) *Romilly's Visits to Wales 1827–1854* (Llandysul: Gomer Press, 1998).

Muller, M. "A few gentlemen of the road" *Pembrokeshire Life*, April (2006).

O'Leary, P. *Immigration and Integration: The Irish in Wales, 1798–1922* (Cardiff: University of Wales Press, 2000).

Owen, H.J. *From Merioneth to Botany Bay* (Dolgellau: Evans, 1952).

Owen, M. "Shame and reparation: womens' place in the kin" in D. Jenkins and M. Owen (eds) *The Welsh Law Of Women* (Cardiff: University of Wales Press, 1980) p. 40.

Owen, M. "Tân: The Welsh law of arson and negligent burning" in T. Charles-Edwards and P. Russell (eds) *Tair Colofn Cyfraith/ The Three Columns of Law in*

Medieval Wales: Homicide, Theft and Fire (Bangor: The Welsh Legal History Society, 2005) p. 108.

Page, A. "The Radnorshire Quarter Sessions, 1773–1873" *The Transactions of The Radnorshire Society* lxxx (2010): 83.

Parker, K. *Parties, Polls and Riots: Politics in Nineteenth-Century Radnorshire* (Woonton Almeley: Logston Press, 2008).

Parry, G. *A Guide to the Records of Great Sessions in Wales* (Aberystwyth: National Library of Wales, 1995).

Parry, G. *Launched to Eternity: Crime and Punishment 1700–1900* (Aberystwyth: National Library of Wales, 2001).

Parry, J. "The Tredegar anti-Irish riots of 1882" *Llafur* 3 (1983): 20.

Parry, R. Gwynedd. "Trosedd a Chosb ym Meirionydd yn Chwedegau Cynnar y Bedwaredd Ganrif ar Bymtheg: Tystiolaeth Cofnodion y Llys Chwarter" in T. Watkin (ed.) *The Trial of Dic Penderyn and Other Essays* (Cardiff: Welsh Legal History Society, 2002) p. 77.

Parry-Jones, D. *Welsh Country Upbringing* (2nd edn, London. B.T. Batsford, 1949).

Patterson, N.W. "Honour and shame in Welsh Society: a study of the role of burlesque in the Welsh Laws" *Studia Celtica* xvi (1981): 73.

Powell, N.M.W. "Crime and the community in Denbighshire during the 1590s: the evidence of the records of the Court of Great Sessions" in J.G Jones (ed.) *Class, Community and Culture in Tudor Wales* (Cardiff: University of Wales Press, 1989) p. 261.

Preece, D. "'Defend the rights of the roads your fathers fought for': the Blaina riot of 1935" *Llafur* (2010): 73.

Pryce, H. *Native Law and the Church in Medieval Wales* (Oxford: Oxford University Press, 1993).

Pryce, H. "Gerald of Wales, Gildas and the Descriptio Kambriae" in F. Edmonds and P. Russell (eds) *Tome: Studies in Medieval Celtic History and Law* (Woodbridge: Boydell Press 2011) p. 115.

Putkowski, J. *The Kinmel Park Riots 1919* (Hawarden: Flintshire Historical Society, 1998).

Rees, A.D. *Life in a Welsh Countryside* (Cardiff: University of Wales Press, 1961).

Rees, E.A. *Welsh Outlaws and Bandits: Political Rebellion and Lawlessness in Wales, 1400–1603* (Birmingham: Caterwen Press, 2001).

Roberts, R.A. (ed.) *The Court Rolls of the Lordship of Ruthin or Dyffryn-Clwyd of the Reign of King Edward I* (London: Nabu Press, 1893).

Roberts, S.E. *The Legal Triads of Medieval Wales* (Cardiff: University of Wales Press, 2007).

Robinson, D. "Crime, police and the provincial press: a study of Victorian Cardiff" *Welsh History Review* 25 (2011): 551.

Rubenstein, W. "The anti-Jewish riots of 1911 in South Wales: a re-examination" *Welsh History Review* 18 (1997): 667.

Rubin, G. "Calling in the Met: Serious crime involving Scotland Yard and provincial police forces in England and Wales, 1906–1939" *Legal Studies* 31 (2011): 411.

Smith, Ll. Beverly "The Statute of Wales 1284" *Welsh History Review* 10 (1980–1981): 127.

Smith, Ll. Beverley "A contribution to the history of galanas in late-medieval Wales" *Studia Celtica* xliii (2009): 87.

Stacey, R.C. *The Road to Judgment: From Custom to Court in Medieval Ireland and Wales* (Philadelphia: University of Pennsylvania Press, 1994).

Stallion, M. and Wall, D.S. *The British Police: Forces and Chief Officers 1829–2012* (2nd edn, Hook: Police History Society, 2011).

Strange, K. "In search of the celestial empire: crime in Merthyr, 1830–60" *Llafur* 3 (1980): 44.

Suggett, R. "The Welsh Language and the Court of Great Sessions" in G. Jenkins (ed.) *The Welsh Language Before The Industrial Revolution* (Cardiff: University of Wales Press, 1997) p. 153.

Suggett, R. *A History of Magic and Witchcraft in Wales* (Stroud: The History Press, 2008).

Taylor, R. *To Catch a Thief* (Chichester: New Wine Press, 2006).

Thomas, N. *The Welsh Extremist: A Culture in Crisis* (London: Lolfa, 1971).

Wallace, R. "'No votes for women, no information from women': the suffragette boycott of the 1911 census in Wales" *Llafur* 11 (2013): 56.

Walters, D.B. "Honour and shame" in N. Cox and T. Watkin (eds) *Canmlwyddiant, Cyfraith a Chymreictod* (Bangor: The Welsh Legal History Society, 2013) p. 229.

Watkin, T.G. *The Legal History of Wales* (2nd edn, Cardiff: University of Wales Press, 2012).

Watson, K. "Women, violent crime and criminal justice in Georgian Wales" *Continuity and Change* 28 (2013): 1.

White, S. "A burial ahead of its time: the Crookenden Burial Case and the sanctioning of cremation in England and Wales" in T. Watkin (ed.) *The Trial of Dic Penderyn and Other Essays* (Cardiff: Welsh Legal History Society, 2002) p. 151.

Wilks, I. *South Wales and the Rising of 1839* (Llandysul: Gomer Press, 1989).

Williams, D. *The Rebecca Riots* (Cardiff: University of Wales Press, 1955).

Williams, G. "Compulsory sterilisation of Welsh miners, 1936" *Llafur* (1982): 67.

Williams, G. "The disenchantment of the world: innovation, crisis and change in Cardiganshire c 1880–1910" *Ceredigion* ix (1983): 303.

Williams, J.R. *Sentenced to Hell: The Story of Men and Women Transported from North Wales 1730–1878* (Pwllheli: Llygad Gwalch Cyf, 2011).

Williams, R. (ed.) *Prison Letters: John Jenkins* (Talybont: Llofa, 1981).

Williams, W.O. *Calendar of the Caernarvonshire Quarter Sessions Vol. 1, 1541–1558* (Caernarfon: Caernarvonshire Historical Society, 1956).

Williams-Jones, K. *A Calendar of the Merioneth Quarter Sessions Rolls Vol. I 1733–1765* (Merioneth: Merioneth County Council, 1965).

Woodward, N. "Burglary in Wales, 1730–1830: evidence from the Great Sessions" *Welsh History Review* 24 (2008): 60.

Woodward, N. "Seasonality and sheep-stealing: Wales 1730–1830" *Agricultural History Review* 56 (2008)3: 25.

Woodward, N. "Horse stealing in Wales 1730–1830" *Agricultural History Review* 57 (2009): 70.

Index